W9-CCN-428

PARENTING TEENAGERS

PARENTING TEENAGERS

A Guide to Solving Problems, Building
Relationships and Creating Harmony in
the Family

JOHN SHARRY

DANVILLE PUBLIC LIBRARY
DANVILLE, INDIANA

VERITAS

Published 2013 by
Veritas Publications
7–8 Lower Abbey Street
Dublin 1
Ireland
publications@veritas.ie
www.veritas.ie

ISBN 978 1 84730 436 0

Copyright © John Sharry, 2013

10 9 8 7 6 5 4 3 2 1

The material in this publication is protected by copyright law. Except
as may be permitted by law, no part of the material may be reproduced
(including by storage in a retrieval system) or transmitted in any form or
by any means, adapted, rented or lent without the written permission of
the copyright owners. Applications for permissions should be addressed
to the publisher.

A catalogue record for this book is available from the British Library.

Designed by Dara O'Connor, Veritas
Printed in Ireland by Hudson Killeen Limited, Dublin

Veritas books are printed on paper made from the wood pulp of managed
forests. For every tree felled, at least one tree is planted, thereby renewing
natural resources.

To Cara, Leo, and Peadar, the greatest loves of my life and also my wisest teachers. Each day I learn something new from you, and love you even more.

ACKNOWLEDGEMENTS

First of all, I would like to acknowledge my wife Grainne in the writing of this book. As co-developer of the Parents Plus programmes, Grainne is one of the most creative clinicians I know, bringing a sensitive understanding of children and young people to the heart of her work. I have the benefit of her creativity and wisdom in any writing that is finally published.

I would also like to thank the Parents Plus team and all my colleagues in the Mater Child and Adolescent Mental Health Service, particularly Carol Fitzpatrick and Eileen Brosnan who co-authored the Parents Plus Adolescents and Working Things Out programmes with me – two great clinicians who are tuned in to the needs of young people.

I am also grateful to Deirdre Veldon of the *Irish Times* for giving me the opportunity to write for the Health and Family supplement. She has always been an encouraging and insightful editor.

Finally, I would like to thank the thousands of parents and young people I have worked with in the last twenty-five years as a mental health professional, and in particular those who had the courage to send in their questions and concerns to the *Irish Times*. It has been a privilege to try to be of service to you and if there is any wisdom in this book, then it is your wisdom.

Contents

GETTING STARTED

This book is for all parents who want to learn ways to help their children and teenagers grow up into happy, secure, well-adjusted and responsible adults. It contains universal principles about what makes family relationships work and how you can help your children navigate the transition from being teenagers to adults. It is particularly for parents who are dealing with challenging behavioural or emotional problems and other difficulties being exhibited by their teenagers, and who are looking for well-researched ideas on how to manage and thrive as a family through these hard times.

Part 1 outlines ten basic principles that provide a step-by-step guide to parenting teenagers and managing teenage problems. The principles build one by one into a comprehensive 'toolkit' for parents that form good habits of positive parenting and which they can draw upon when faced by any teenage problem.

Part 2 is written in a question and answer format and features thirty of my columns from the *Irish Times* Health and Family supplement. All the columns are based on questions and concerns that were sent in by readers and so represent the most common and current concerns of parents of older children and teenagers.

There are a number of ways to read this book. You can read through each chapter from beginning to end or you can start with the problem that most concerns you in Part 2, and then go back to the principles and steps in Part 1. It is possible to read Part 1 as a step-by-step guide that you can apply in your family over a period of weeks, applying one principle at a time before returning to the book for the next. The key to making the ideas work is to try them out at home and to test them through your own experience. At the end of each chapter there are specific tips for putting the principles into action.

While the ideas should prove useful to most families, none can apply in every situation and in every context. Each family is different and it is parents who know their own children and their families best. I encourage you to reflect on what works for you as a parent and to adapt the ideas and suggestions to your unique family situation. While I encourage you to try new things, trust your instinct to lead you to what's best for you and your family.

You will notice that throughout this book you are encouraged to build on your teenager's strengths and abilities. Apply the same principles to yourself. Too often parents give themselves a hard time, criticising their own behaviour and putting themselves down. I encourage you to break this negative pattern and reverse it. Start looking for what you and your partner are doing right as parents. Be on the lookout for the small steps of improvement each day, the times you manage successfully, and begin to notice what you are grateful for as a parent.

It is in your children's interests that you identify your own strengths and successes. Children learn a powerful lesson from you when you model self-encouragement. They learn how to be confident and successful and how to relate positively to other people. Remember, the goal is not to be a perfect parent or to have a perfect child. Such people do not exist (and if they did they would be unbearable to be around). Rather, the goal is to be a 'good enough' parent – someone who accepts themselves, appreciates their own strengths and weaknesses, tries their best and learns from experience.

Many of the ideas herein are drawn from the Parents Plus Adolescents programme – an evidence-based parenting course developed by the Parents Plus Charity in the Mater Hospital Child and Adolescent Mental Health Service, in partnership with parents and young people. The Parents Plus programmes are delivered by professional facilitators in services throughout Ireland, the UK and further afield. The principles focus on well-researched ideas about what makes family relationships work, how best to communicate and solve problems, as well as behaviour management principles and discipline. Most of the ideas will be familiar to you and be recognised as positive habits of parenting to which we all aspire. For more information on the Parents Plus programmes and their evidence base, please go to www.parentsplus.ie.

PART 1
Ten Steps to Positive Parenting for Teenagers

INTRODUCTION: BECOMING A PARENT OF A TEENAGER: A STORMY TIME

He just doesn't listen anymore and is so secretive and moody. He thinks that we [his parents] are for the birds and just wants to be with his friends all the time.

She's become so argumentative and abusive. Anytime we ask her to do anything, she starts world war three in the house.

I don't feel as close to her anymore, she seems to have her own life without me.

Becoming the parent of a teenager can be a troubled time. The open child who chatted happily to you might have suddenly transformed into an argumentative and resentful teenager who challenges everything you say. Teenagers can become secretive and suspicious, and parents can feel redundant and locked out of their lives. In addition, you can be full of fears for your teenager. There are so many pressures on teenagers to become involved in drugs and alcohol or to become sexually active at too young an age. With their increasing independence, you fear for their safety, worrying that they might be attacked or placed in dangerous situations. It can be a struggle to set boundaries and limits with a teenager who may resent your authority as a parent.

Parents are usually in their forties or fifties when their children become teens and may be going through their own life changes. At this stage of life parents are often wondering about the direction of their own lives and careers, sometimes feeling that life has passed them by. Having teenagers who seem to have endless opportunities and who appear ungrateful can stir up a lot of emotion in parents, even causing them to feel envious. Alternatively parents may be looking forward to a quieter period in their life, only for this to be rudely disturbed by a noisy and demanding teenager. In this context, it is understandable for parents to react negatively to this stormy period, to lose sight of the bigger picture and miss out on the enjoyable aspects of parenting a teenager.

It's Difficult for Teenagers Too

The transition from child to adult is difficult for teenagers. So many changes occur in these short years that it is not surprising they feel confused, frightened and unconfident at times. They can be subject to significant mood swings as they discover the range of human emotions; from intense feelings of love and infatuation to anger and hatred, teenage emotional life can be like a rollercoaster. Their bodies grow and change in ways that might make them feel awkward and self-conscious. The physical development that occurs during the teenage years can lead to intense sexual feelings, which can be alarming, especially if they have no one to talk to about what is going on. Yet teenagers also make great gains intellectually, becoming more analytical and developing their own opinions and views; they begin to see the inadequacies in the parental world (and often are very eloquent in pointing this out!), and wonder about their role and meaning in life.

Teenagers are under numerous pressures, some of which are greater than they have been in the past, and need the support of their parents more than ever.

Navigating Through the Teenage Storm

When facing the crisis of the teenage years many parents react by trying to take control. They may become authoritarian and strict, battling with their teenagers to ensure they tow the line. Other parents avoid their teenagers' problems and back down from every conflict, effectively giving up on trying to influence them or being involved in their life. Both approaches are problematic: the young person with authoritarian parents may rebel even more, escalating the conflict, or they may go 'underground' with their problems, hiding more things from their parents. The teenager with permissive parents may feel uncared for and neglected, and without parental supervision become involved in unsafe behaviours. Both approaches rob teenagers of having parents who can support them through the difficulties they face.

This book aims to describe a 'middle-way' approach to parenting that shows how you can stay supportively involved in your teenager's life, while also being firm enough to ensure they learn to take responsibility for their actions. The aim is to help teenagers grow into confident adults, who are separate and independent but also appropriately connected to their family and able to form their own intimate relationships in the future.

Many writers describe family life, and especially parenting a teenager, as being like embarking on a plane journey together. With a young child, the parent is in the pilot's seat navigating the plane and in charge of the controls. As a child gets older, a good parent allows the child into the cockpit and begins to teach him how to operate the controls. As the child becomes a teenager, he begins to take the first steps of flying his own plane. The parent's role now becomes the important one of 'co-pilot', with the teenager slowly trying out his new skills. The co-pilot is there for the teenager, offering encouragement and guidance, letting him learn from mistakes and achievements, teaching him slowly how to become a responsible pilot. Often this is difficult for families. Many parents fear that the child will not be able to fly safely and battle to take back the controls. Other parents do not give children any lessons at all, letting them learn the skills of flying from other people, such as school friends or from television or online. However, a good parent realises that the aim of the journey is to teach the teenager how to fly his own plane in the future and that it is far better that he learns this with his parents as supportive, involved co-pilots.

A Time of Opportunity

While acknowledging the potential strife and difficulties in bringing up a teenager, this book also suggests that parents seek out the positive and brighter side of parenting a teenager. Rather than seeing the teenage years as problem years, try and see them as full of opportunity. During these years parents have the opportunity to form a different relationship with their child, one that is more adult and equal. Teenage rebellion is not a personal attack on your authority but a necessary stage for teenagers to go through as they forge their separate identity. If you remain curious and interested in this process you can help them think through their values and ideas. By staying involved in your teenager's life, you can get to know them in a different way – as young adults rather than children. Many parents report how satisfying it can be to begin having adult conversations with their teenagers. In addition, by staying involved you can share in their achievements and discoveries as they mature. You can appreciate and enjoy their excitement as they face a world full of opportunity, and have the pleasure of providing support as they take on the world. In the difficult times try and remember that parenting is a long-term task. By staying involved and being firm when needed you can chart a course through the hard times so that you can be there as your teenagers grow into young adults of whom you can be proud.

STEP 1: PRESSING THE PAUSE BUTTON

It's the last straw for Pete when his fourteen-year-old son arrives home hours late after specifically promising to be in on time. Pete confronts him angrily, asking, 'Where the hell have you been?' The son, in return, becomes defensive and angry and tells his father to mind his own business. The confrontation escalates and the son storms off to his room. Pete is left wondering what has happened between them.

Teenagers are at a time of life when they are separating from their parents. They are becoming their own people with different ideas and values. Though this is healthy, it can bring them into conflict with their parents and lead to a stormy time for all. As discussed in the last section, this period can be hard for parents. Teenagers can become challenging and demanding. At times they can be disrespectful and even abusive to their parents. It is not surprising that parents, hurt and bewildered by these exchanges, can react negatively by criticising, lecturing, rowing and even lashing out at their teenagers. This can lead to unpleasant scenes, like that described above, leaving both teenager and parent upset and hurt.

Pressing the Pause Button

So how can a parent handle this conflict? How can you stop things from escalating to a full-blown row? The first thing you can do is press the pause button. Rather than reacting to a situation or flying off the handle, pause and ask yourself the following questions:

» What is the best way to manage this situation?
» What way do I want to respond?
» What result do I want?

In conflictual situations, pressing the pause button may mean taking a deep breath and calming down when you feel yourself getting angry or about to react to a situation. It can be best not to continue the argument, which may lead to hurtful things being said, and to set a time later to talk things through when everyone is calmer. Consider how Pete in the example above might have pressed the pause button:

> *When his son came in late, Pete found himself getting very angry but quickly noticed this. He took a deep breath and said, 'Look son, I'm just too upset and angry to talk now. Go to your room and we will talk tomorrow.' The son went off in a huff, but a serious row was averted. Pete collected himself, thinking about the best way to deal with his son's lateness. He decided on a way and then sat down with him at a later time when they were both calm.*

WHEN TEENAGERS ARE DISRESPECTFUL

Pressing the pause button can also be helpful when teenagers become abusive and disrespectful to parents. Rather than tolerating the teenager's abuse or responding with a few choice words of your own, you can 'pause the row' by refusing to participate anymore and waiting for a better time to resolve the conflict. Consider the example below:

> *When Alice asked her daughter to stay in one evening, she exploded abusively, telling her mother to 'back off' and 'stop messing up her life'. Though Alice was hurt and tempted to respond angrily, she pressed the pause button. She calmly said, 'Look, I'm not happy with you speaking to me in this way. When you can talk civilly then I'll listen.' The daughter continued to protest and Alice repeated what she had just said and walked away. By stepping away from the situation, Alice could think about what to do and her daughter had space to calm down. An hour later her daughter approached her and the two of them sat down to talk. Alice calmly explained how hurt she was and the daughter apologised. Together they negotiated a compromise about going out.*

By pressing the pause button, Alice nipped the argument in the bud and avoided the row escalating to a point where hurtful and damaging things might be said. By not returning her daughter's abuse, Alice not only made it more likely that a constructive conversation could take place later, but she also taught her daughter an important lesson about how to remain respectful and calm in a difficult situation.

DON'T WAIT FOR A ROW, PRESS THE PAUSE BUTTON IN ADVANCE!
You don't have to wait until you are in the middle of a row to press the pause button and think through how you want to manage a conflict or how you want to be as a parent. In fact, the more often you sit down (either by yourself or with your partner or a trusted friend) to reflect on your parenting and to plan how you are going to handle situations, the better things are likely to be for yourself and your family. Good planning and communication can avoid many problems. For example, by taking time to plan the family holiday with your teenagers, a choice can be made that meets the preferences of everyone, preventing a disastrous trip full of rows and conflict.

However, many parents caught up in busy schedules don't give themselves thinking time or forget to plan things with their family. The purpose of this book is to make room for that thinking time in your busy parenting schedule. Most of the exercises and suggestions are about pressing the pause button by yourself or with your children in order to think and talk about how you want to be as a family. The following are some pointers you might like to remember in reflecting on how to approach problems with your teens:

1. Focus on your goal and what you want to happen (what way do you want to be as a parent, couple, family?).
2. Focus on what you can do. Rather than waiting for your teenager to change, what can you do to help them change or make the situation better?
3. Remember what has worked with your teenager in the past (for example, you may remember that chatting after dinner is more effective) and try to do this again.
4. If something isn't working, try something different.

PRESSING THE PAUSE BUTTON IN ADVANCE: EXAMPLES

» Rather than being authoritarian when her son refused to do something, Jean decided to take some time to listen to his point of view and try to reach a compromise.

» Arthur realised that it was a bad time to harangue his daughter with questions about school the minute she came in the door and remembered that a better time was later, after dinner, when everyone was relaxed.

» Instead of jumping in to referee when his two sons got into a squabble, Roy decided to back off, saying to them, 'Listen, the two of you are old enough to sort your disagreements out.'

» Julie used to constantly nag her daughter to clean her room, to no avail. She decided to pay no attention to it anymore, but told her daughter that she would only get her full pocket money if she cleaned her room.

Tips for the Future

1. Press the pause button when faced by rows and arguments. Step back and think, 'How do I want to respond?'

2. Think of a particular problem that occurs in your family and plan what you might do to make a difference.

3. Sit down and make a list of goals. What way do you want to be as a parent, as a couple, as a family? What is important? Maybe start a discussion with others in the family.

STEP 2: CONNECTING WITH YOUR TEENAGER

When my children got older, I felt redundant. They had their own friends and lives. It became harder to understand them.

Parents Matter

Often parents have the sense of being out of touch with their teenager. Teenagers get caught up with their own friends and interests, and it is easy to feel distant from them and that you don't matter to them any more. Yet teenagers still really need their parents, parents who remain involved and interested in their lives. Though they are growing up and separating from the family, they still need support, guidance and encouragement. Young people need adults who can be there to act as their co-pilot as they negotiate any problems. If you are unsure about the importance of your role in your teenager's life, you only have to consider the extensive research showing that teenagers whose parents stay connected and supportively involved in their lives are much more likely to grow into healthy, successful adults with fewer problems. Researchers have also found that, for example, children whose parents discuss the issue of drugs with them are 36 per cent less likely to experiment with drugs than children who do not have these discussions with their parents.

Staying involved in your teenager's life is not about knowing everything about them or learning things so you can control them. Teenagers need their privacy and distance, and it would be inappropriate for them to reveal all the personal details of their lives to their parents. Rather, having a connection with teenagers is about knowing the things in life which are important to them, such as the names of their friends, their routine at school, the position of their team in the league, what their favourite dinner is, and so on. When you know these mundane and ordinary details about your teenagers, not only does it mean that you are sharing in their lives, but it gives you an opportunity to positively influence them about other important matters, such as drugs and safety.

Building a Connection with your Teenager

So how do you get through to teenagers? How do you reach out to them when they appear withdrawn and moody? This is not always easy, as there can be a sizable gap between parents and teenagers in terms of interests and concerns. Building a good relationship with your teenager takes effort; it is not something that can be done overnight, but rather is the result of careful emotional investment of time and energy. There are a number of ideas that can help.

SET TIME ASIDE TO BE WITH YOUR TEENAGER

Building a connection with your teenager is not something that can be rushed or fitted into a busy schedule. The most important decision you can make is to set time aside when you can talk and be with your teenager in a relaxed way. This does not have to be a special activity or trip (though these can help, as we shall see in Step 3). Ordinary activities – such as watching TV together, the drive to school, mealtimes and doing the washing up together – can all act as times when you can chat to one another.

> *Rob found the drive to work in the morning when he dropped his son to school a real stress. They would always be late and tempers could become frayed in the traffic. As a result he changed his schedule so they had more time in the morning. This made the journey more relaxing, giving them time to spend together either chatting or listening to the radio. It became a time they both looked forward to.*

Some parents find routine events are particularly helpful times to talk and listen to their children, such as when they come in from school, at mealtimes, or just before they go to bed. Many families agree to make some of these times special, such as making an effort to get together for Sunday dinner.

GET TO KNOW SPECIFIC DETAILS ABOUT YOUR TEENAGER'S WORLD

Parents who are involved in their children's lives know countless ordinary details about what is important to them. They take an interest in their hobbies and make a point of remembering their friends' names. They are curious about what their children think and feel about things, especially things that are important to them. Gaining this knowledge of your child's life takes time, but it really shows in the quality of interaction between parent and child. Consider the example below:

Joan would make a special effort to be available to her children when they came in from school. She would stop any work she was doing and sit down with her children over a cup a tea. She made sure there would be time and space for everyone to say how their day went. Joan made a point to ask specifically what went on for them during the day and she always remembered to ask about important things such as football matches or trips. This special time after school became a really important family ritual that Joan and the children looked forward to.

BE ENCOURAGING

Teenagers are often insecure and struggling with many pressures at school and from friends. The argumentative or sulky moods are only a front and they need more than ever the support and encouragement of their parents. It is important that you do this in a genuine way, as teenagers will be the first to shrug off any attention they consider to be fake or manipulative. Generally, encouragement works best with teenagers if it is matter of fact rather than over the top, and if it is specific (whereby you clearly name what you are pleased about and how you feel about it). Remember, each teenager is different; what gets through with one teenager will not work for another. What is important is that you find a way of providing encouragement to your teenager about routine, everyday activities. Giving compliments to teenagers in a genuine way that gets through to them can make a difference.

BE ENCOURAGING: EXAMPLES

» Noticing if your teenager tries harder at schoolwork.
» Casually thanking your teenager when he does a chore rather than taking it for granted.

» Complimenting teenagers on their appearance or what they're wearing.

Going out of our way to look for positive things does not come easily to most of us. We are not used to it and praise can be hard to give, particularly when there has been conflict or things have not been going well with a child for some time. But that is probably the most important time to be positive and notice even small signs of improvement. For example, if your teenager is normally grumpy with visitors, but on one occasion behaves more positively, you could say: 'I appreciate it when you talk with my friends, it means a lot to me when you take an interest.' Or if a teenager who normally gets into a row with his sister walks away instead, you could say: 'I was impressed with how you handled things with your sister earlier. You didn't get wound up and avoided a row.'

RESPONDING TO YOUR TEENAGER'S INITIATIVE

One of the greatest opportunities to connect with your teenager is to respond to any initiative they take to talk or connect with you. Often they choose inopportune times, when you're busy or tired or just about to go out and do something yourself. However, in these situations it's worth weighing up what is most important – the tasks you're busy with or your relationship with your teenager. While you can sometimes postpone responding to your teenager, it can be really helpful to respond there and then, especially if your teenager does not usually open up or try to make a connection with you. It can be a case of making sure to seize the opportunity. Consider the following examples:

» If your son asks for help with homework and you're busy, try and give a little bit of time and then set aside another time to help further.

» If your daughter suddenly opens up one night because her boyfriend split up with her, this might be a time to postpone going to bed to stay up and listen.

» If your son wants to watch a favourite TV programme and you're reading, it might be a good idea to postpone your reading and watch the programme with him.
» If your daughter asks you a personal question when you're reading the newspaper, you can put down the newspaper for a few minutes and try to listen and answer the question.
» If your son asks you for a lift, rather than lecturing him about not being his chauffeur, use the journey as an opportunity to talk to and listen to him.

Tips for the Future

1. Set aside a relaxed time to talk with your teenager, when the two of you can sit and chat.
2. Make a list of all the specific details you know about your teenager (their friends, interests, school, what they like/dislike etc.) and make an effort to fill any gaps you notice by taking a real interest in your teenager's life. (Remember, your teenager may only open up slowly.)
3. Be really encouraging of your teenager. Go out of your way to notice any things they do that you like or you're proud of and make sure to tell them this.
4. Make sure to respond to any times your teen attempts to connect with or talk to you.

STEP 3: GETTING TO KNOW YOUR TEENAGER

Being a Teenager

As a parent it's easy to forget what it is like to be a teenager. You can find yourself being critical of the younger generation, complaining about their laziness or lack of respect for older people. You can see their moodiness as a burden and something you can't understand. However, what young people really need is their parents' understanding. Teenagers are often very critical of themselves, feeling awkward and having low self-esteem. They need to know that you are on their side. To appreciate what it is like to be in your teenager's shoes, it can help to remember what it was like for you when you were growing up. To do this I suggest you take a few minutes with the following exercise.

REMEMBERING BEING A TEENAGER

1. Take a few moments out of your routine so that you can think and reflect.
2. Close your eyes and take a few deep breaths to relax.
3. Begin to recall what it was like when you were ten or eleven years old. Pick out specific events or people that signify that time for you. Focus on recalling specific details (how you were feeling, what people were saying, what things looked like then etc.).
4. When you're ready, begin to move forward in time to when you were fifteen or sixteen and begin to recall what things were like for you then. Once again, recall specific events and people in as much detail as possible.
5. When you are ready, move forward again to the present day and back to the room you're in.
6. Think about what you noticed about your 'journey' through time. It can help to write things down in a journal or talk to someone, such as your partner, about what you have remembered. This can be a good exercise to do as a couple.

This exercise can be very powerful in getting you in touch with your own teenage years. It can be a difficult exercise as you might recall sad memories, or it can be mixed as you recall good and bad memories. As a parent doing the exercise, it can make you realise some of the issues that your own teenager is going through. Though there are many differences between being a teenager nowadays and a generation ago (for example, it is true to say teenagers have more freedom and there is wider availability of drugs), many of the issues are the same. By remembering these common issues and concerns you have made another step in understanding and connecting with your teenager.

WHAT TEENAGERS THINK ABOUT

So what do teenagers think about? What issues are important to them and what concerns press upon their minds? Below are the sorts of worries that teenagers have reported as concerning them most:

1. Will I make friends or will anyone like me?
2. Will anyone fancy me or ask me out?
3. How come I don't fit in with others?
4. What should I do about drugs and alcohol?
5. Will I do all right in the class exams?
6. Will I ever get a decent job?
7. What should I do with my life?
8. How can I please my parents/get them off my back?

Teenagers also tend to have strong views about how they should be parented and about what they want from their parents:

1. They want their parents to trust them and have faith in them.
2. They want privacy. They want to talk to their parents about some things but they don't want to tell them everything.
3. They want to be treated fairly. Justice and fair play are really important to them.

Getting to Know Your Teenager

As a parent, the best thing you can do to be a positive influence in your teenager's life is to go out of your way to understand them and to know their world. Rules and discipline require teenagers to cooperate voluntarily, and thus are only possible when you have established a good relationship. Below are a number of things you can do to make a difference to your relationship with your teenager.

BE INTERESTED

Be genuinely interested in your teenagers and all they do. You want to know them, not because you want to control them, but because you genuinely want to get to know their world. You want to know their opinions and feelings. You want to understand why they love computer games so much or what they enjoy about football, so you can share in this with them. This often requires suspending your critical judgements of their interests and hobbies and reaching out to understand them. For example, rather than always criticising a TV programme your daughter watches, make an effort to suspend judgement, watch it with her and then debate the issues it raises, listening to her point of view first. Let your teenager teach you about their interests and what it is like to be living in the teenage world. See yourself as a curious but respectful traveller in the foreign land of adolescence, not a critical tourist! Instead of simply restricting your son's use of the internet, let him teach you all the benefits and opportunities it provides. By learning about it yourself you are in a better position to open a debate about the problems of safety or excessive use. You may be surprised that your teenager has already thought about many of the issues involved. Your job then becomes one of a supportive coach, helping him to think things through and make decisions.

SPEND ONE-TO-ONE TIME WITH YOUR TEENAGER

The best way to build a close relationship with your teenager is to ensure you have one-to-one quality time with them, when the two of you are together with no interruptions. While this can be difficult with teenagers who appear disinterested in spending time with their parents and parents who are busy with their own lives, time alone with your teenager is still the best way to get to know them and stay involved with their life. There are many things you can do to achieve this and often it is best to plan in advance to find activities that you both enjoy doing together.

» Watching a favourite TV programme
» Doing homework
» Shopping together
» Playing cards
» Playing sport
» Baking/cooking
» Walking the dog

» Following a sports team
» Making something (e.g. a craft)
» Walking or cycling
» Camping
» Doing a course together
» Fishing
» Working on the computer

MAKE THE DECISION TO GET TO KNOW YOUR TEENAGER

Getting to know your teenager isn't something that just happens. The generation gap can be quite large and requires an effort on the part of the parent to bridge it. This is especially the case when parents feel out of touch with their teenagers or if there has been a lot of conflict. Consider the two examples below:

Richard found his fourteen-year-old son particularly grumpy and moody and he felt out of touch with him. So he looked to find an activity they could do together. The son was really interested in football though Richard thought it was a waste of time. But he decided to take an interest in football and began to attend matches with his son. Slowly he discovered and begun to share his son's love for the sport. The weekly football trip soon became their regular weekend outing and a real bond between them.

Sue found herself in constant battles with her daughter over schoolwork. She was worried that they had nothing in common. However, when she thought about it she remembered that they both shared an interest in films. So as a treat she planned a special movie night, where the two of them would select a movie and go together and round off the evening in a coffee shop. This worked well as during the meal they always had a great chat about the movie and other things.

BE PREPARED TO SHARE YOUR OWN EXPERIENCES

Generally, teenagers love when parents are prepared to share their own honest feelings and experiences rather than just give lectures. For example, rather than preaching to a teenager about the virtues of hard work in school or about the issues surrounding teenage sex, maybe share with them your own personal struggles in school or your own teenage worries about relationships. It might be helpful to share the results of the remembering exercise at the beginning of this section with your teenager. Sharing your own feelings and experiences can be really helpful in improving your relationship with your teenager. Consider the example from a mother below:

I was always concerned about my daughter not studying and going out all the time and this would lead to a lot of conflict. Things changed when we were away together one weekend and I told her honestly about my own school experience. I had been taken out of school early by my parents to work and always resented not having the opportunity to go to college. Talking to her made me realise how part of my pressure on my daughter was to do with my own lack of fulfilment. My daughter was very understanding when I told her this and she opened up about the pressures she had in school, which were different than mine. We began to understand one another and have become much closer as a result.

SPEND FAMILY TIME TOGETHER

Another way to get to know your teenager is to ensure there are regular times when the whole family spends quality time together. This can include special activities, such as a day trip, going on a picnic or staying in for a special movie night. Many families organise a special family night (usually following a family meeting – see Step 9) where everyone stays in, perhaps to share a meal, play games, tell stories, play music or simply spend time with one another.

Tips for the Future

1. Plan to do an activity or take up a hobby you can share with your teenager.
2. Plan an enjoyable family event or set aside family time when you do something that everyone, including your teenagers, can enjoy and take part in.

STEP 4: COMMUNICATING EFFECTIVELY – LISTENING AND SPEAKING UP

Active Listening

Most parents agree that listening to their children is really important. Some experts in the field actually rate listening as *the* most important parenting skill of all. This is because it helps parents understand their teenagers and also helps resolve conflict, allowing them to carry out discipline effectively. Yet despite this, very few of us get any training in how to listen. Sometimes we can find it very hard, especially when we have strong views about what we want for our teenagers.

Active listening involves great effort. It involves stepping out of your own shoes into those of another person. It involves moving to see the world as they see it and to appreciate the feelings they have towards it. It is about going that extra distance to understand their point of view. When your child does something you strongly disagree with, a good indicator that you have understood empathetically is an appreciation that you might have committed the same error if you had been in their shoes or faced the same set of circumstances.

SO, HOW DO YOU ACTIVELY LISTEN?

Active listening is very different than the many other ways we might communicate with teenagers, such as giving advice, criticising or coaching (all useful skills at times, but not when we are attempting to understand a child's feelings). Consider the following responses to a teenager:

Teenager (upset): James just turned the TV over to another channel.
Parent: Well, I'm sure it was his turn. (*Arguing*)
You shouldn't be watching so much TV. (*Criticising*)
Why don't you just do something else? (*Advising*)
Oh don't worry, it's not so bad. (*Coaching*)
Let me go and talk to James. (*Rescuing*)

Instead, active listening is something quite different. It involves the following skills:

» Genuinely trying to understand.
» Acknowledging what the other person is feeling.
» Repeating what the other person has said, to check you have understood.
» Giving full attention via your body language and eye contact.
» Encouraging the other person to continue by nodding, being silent, repeating the last word they have said, asking gentle questions etc.

Now consider some alternative listening responses:

Teenager (upset): James just turned the TV over to another channel.
Parent: Sounds like you're upset. Sit down and tell me what happened. (*Picking up on feelings and encouraging child to say more*)
I'm sorry, I know how much you like watching that programme. (*Acknowledging feelings*)

In the above examples the parent is validating the child's feelings and attempting to see the problem from his point of view. Sometimes simply repeating what the child has said or nodding encouragingly can be sufficient to help the child feel listened to and to encourage him to express more.

It is important to remember that good listening can't be reduced to a set of techniques. (If you do find yourself 'parroting' techniques, your teenager will soon point this out to you.) What counts is your genuine attempt to understand and appreciate the other's point of view. You have listened effectively when the other person feels understood and that you haven't judged them and are on their side.

LISTENING CHANGES YOU
When we listen empathetically to another person we open ourselves up to being influenced by them. We allow ourselves to be changed and

transform the nature of our relationship with the other person. Consider the following example from a father:

> *I always considered myself to have a good relationship with my two teenage sons. I thought everyone enjoyed the joking and good-natured banter that would go on between us. That was until the younger of the two exploded one day over very little. I gave him what for, but I could see something was really bugging him so I went back to him and listened. He told me how he had always felt embarrassed and humiliated by the banter and the teasing. I began to hear how this had really damaged him. I can't tell you how painful this was to hear, but it marked a pivotal point in our relationship. One year on, we have a much closer and adult relationship. I can't tell you how glad I am I decided to listen that day.*

Speaking Up

We've talked about the importance of actively listening to teenagers when they feel strongly about something. It is equally important that parents communicate their own feelings when they feel strongly about something. Teenagers need parents who don't go along with everything they say. They need parents who are prepared to state their own views and to communicate their own values and opinions. However, how this is done makes a big difference. Skilled communicators always *listen first* before speaking up with their own point of view. Often people get the order of this wrong: they attempt to get their point of view across before listening to the other person. This can lead to a lot of conflict. When we understand another person's point of view and have acknowledged their feelings, they are far more likely to be open to listen to us in return. Expressing your views and concerns also requires skill and tact. Often parents fall into the traps of blaming, criticising or not acknowledging their own feelings. Speaking up respectfully involves:

1. Remaining calm and positive
2. Taking responsibility for your feelings by using an 'I' message. For example, 'I feel upset', rather than 'you made me upset'.

3. Expressing your positive intentions and concerns, such as 'I want you to be safe.'
4. Focusing on what you want to happen. For example saying, 'I want you to tell me when you're going to be late.'

EXAMPLES OF INEFFECTIVE AND EFFECTIVE SPEAKING UP

Ineffective: What the hell do you think you are playing at staying out so late? You've really upset me. *(Attacking and blaming 'you' message)*

Effective: I worry about you going out late at night, especially when it is dark. You see, I want you to be safe.
(Expresses feelings as a positive concern using an 'I' message)

Ineffective: Is there something wrong with you that you don't see this mess? You and your friends are so inconsiderate. *(Sarcastic, blaming)*

Effective: Listen, I like it when your friends come round, but I get frustrated if they leave the place in a mess. I'd really like it if they tidied up after themselves. *(States positive first, acknowledges own feelings of frustration and then makes a clear reasonable request)*

Ineffective: You're talking rubbish now. Of course it's always wrong for teenagers at school to get involved in a sexual relationship. *(Argumentative, attacking)*

Effective: My own view is that teenagers at school are far too young to get involved in a sexual relationship. *(Respectful offering of parent's view and personal values)*

Tips for the Future

1. Practice communicating well with your teenagers and other family members. When they feel strongly about something, make a real attempt to actively listen and to understand their point of view.
2. Practice speaking up respectfully to your teenager, offering your view in a calm and assertive way.

STEP 5: MANAGING CONFLICT

Fifteen-year-old Lisa arrives home from school one day and drops the bombshell that she's had enough and has decided to leave school. Her father, Bill, who is just home after a stressful day at work, flies off the handle, saying she's talking nonsense, that she is far too young to even consider leaving school. Lisa storms off, slamming the door, saying she's going to leave anyway.

Conflicts such as the one described above are common in families with teenagers or older children. Teenagers are on route to becoming independent from their parents and this can be a long process, with each 'step of independence' being hard fought for, as parent and child clash over rules. Adolescence is the time of life when young people need to separate and be different from their parents – they will often have different views on clothes, time-keeping, friends, money, the importance of school work and so on. Though it can lead to conflict, the expression of these different views is healthy and helps young people grow up into confident adults. What is important is how conflict is managed in families. You want to have a family where there is a healthy and respectful expression of differences, but you do not want excessive conflict leading to constant rows as this can make things worse and damage relationships.

In this section we look at how, as a parent, you can manage conflict between yourself and your teenager in a way that is respectful and positive and which allows for the possibility to resolve the cause of the problems. We review ideas already covered, and consider how these can be applied specifically to resolving conflict:

1. Pressing the Pause Button
2. Active Listening
3. Speaking Up Assertively

PRESSING THE PAUSE BUTTON

The behaviour of teenagers can be very provocative and challenging at times. In working out their own views, teenagers may reject values or ideas that are very important to their parents. For example, if you are a religious person, your teenager may refuse to go to church; or if cooking is important to you, your teenager might reject your food and choose an 'alternative diet'; or if education is important to you, your teenager may threaten to drop out of school. Teenagers can know what buttons to push to get you going and this can cause great conflict. However, the first step to combat this is to press your own pause button. Rather than reacting angrily, take some time out to understand what is going on. Instead of taking your teenager's behaviour personally, understand it as part of their growing up into being adults. Remember, if you do resort to lecturing, or angry exchanges, you may inadvertently fan the flames of the rebellion.

Pressing the pause button gives you time to think through the best way to respond. Even if there has been a row or if you have overreacted, pressing the pause button gives you an opportunity to apologise and start again. In the example at the beginning of this section, Bill could recover after the row by taking some time for himself to consider what is going on, then approaching Lisa at a later time apologising for flying off the handle, and finally asking her to start again and tell him what happened.

Learning to pause before you speak is about keeping the important rule of respect in mind, which will be discussed in more detail in Steps 7 and 8. This rule applies to teenagers as well as parents. If you find your teen getting too angry and disrespectful, be prepared to interrupt the conversation and ask for respect: 'I appreciate that you are upset, but you must talk politely.'

ACTIVE LISTENING

In conflict situations between parent and teenager, emotions are likely to be running high. Conflicts are at their worst when both feel really strongly, but differently, about something. In the above example, Lisa may be feeling really hopeless about school, thinking it is of no benefit to her. Her father, on the other hand, may believe that teenagers should finish school, and may fear the prospect of her leaving early. In the context of their strong but different feelings, it is understandable that Bill might get angry and Lisa might storm off. However, until they find a way of listening to one another they are unlikely to resolve the disagreement.

Active listening isn't easy. It is especially hard when there is serious conflict, such as that between Bill and Lisa. However, these are the times when active listening is especially useful. If you don't listen, the conflict doesn't disappear, in fact it may worsen, as your teenager is likely to feel hurt and not open up about what is really going on for them. Consider the continuation of Bill and Lisa's exchange below, in which Bill goes out of his way to listen to his daughter's feelings and to understand her point of view:

Bill: (*Pauses and takes a deep breath*) Look, I'm sorry. Let me try and understand.

Lisa: School is wrecking my head. I'm always in trouble. Even when I try the teachers don't notice.

Bill: I see.

Lisa: Yeah, each day I go in I feel they're picking on me. I'd be better off leaving and getting work.

Bill: You've been having a real hard time at school recently.

Lisa: Yeah, I have. (*Bill silently nods and puts arm around his daughter's shoulder. Lisa shows a small response, suggesting she is beginning to feel understood*)

Lisa: That's why I want to leave. I'd be much better leaving and getting a job somewhere. (*Pause*)

Bill: Right … I don't think I've appreciated how much of a struggle school has been for you. I guess because I've always wanted it to go well for you. I need to think about what you are saying. Can we talk later? Because this is a very important issue.

Lisa: Yeah.

In the above conversation, Bill is making a real attempt to listen to his daughter, but it is hard for him to take on board his daughter's struggles in school and thus her wish to leave, probably because these views run counter to his strongly held opinion about the importance of completing education. However, if he truly wants to support his daughter's education he has to become her ally. He has to first hear about his daughter's difficulties in school before he can go on to help her solve the problem. (In Step 9 we will look at possible ways of developing solutions.) When your teenager feels strongly about something, these are really opportunities in disguise. By listening well at these times you have the opportunity to connect deeply with your teenager and to transform your relationship with them.

SPEAKING UP ASSERTIVELY

While listening is usually the best way to begin resolving a conflict, it is also important for parents to speak up and communicate their own point of view. However, how this is done makes a real difference. It is important that you don't come across as aggressive by intimidating or inadvertently attacking your teenager. It is equally important that you do not remain passive, keeping quiet for fear of upsetting your teenager, or by backing down too easily and letting your teenager walk all over you. Rather, the aim is to speak up assertively, communicating respectfully and calmly what you feel and think and making sure to express your positive intentions and feelings.

Even during serious conflicts between parent and child, active listening and speaking up assertively are the best way to begin to resolve them. Consider the next example, in which a mother tackles her son over the drugs she has found in his room. She has taken time to think about what she going to say and has picked a good time to approach him to discuss what she has found:

Mother: Look, I've something very important to talk to you about.
Son: What?
Mother: I found this in your room (*Sets what looks like cannabis on the table. Son looks shocked*)
Mother: I know it's cannabis.
Son: (Outraged) What the hell were you doing in my room?
Mother: (Calm) I was worried because you've been behaving out of

character lately, so I decided to check.

Son: You had no right to go into my room.

Mother: (Respectfully) I'm sorry, but I needed to find out what was going on.

Son: (Slumps in chair) Well, it's none of your business.

Mother: It's because I'm very worried for you. I don't want you to use drugs.

Son: It's only hash. It's no big deal.

Mother: It is a big deal to me. I want you to be safe and well. *(Folds arms)*

Mother: Listen to me. *(Teen turns)* We are going to have to talk about this and sort it out. *(The son sighs and sort of gives in, as if he's beginning to sense parents persistent concern for him)*

In this example the mother speaks up firmly and well. She has clearly thought through what she was going to say. Though it was a serious and worrying issue, she remained calm. She expressed her feelings clearly and positively, stating her concern for her son. Finally, she did not take the bait in rising to his son's anger and was persistent in getting her positive message through.

In Summary

Managing conflict is essentially about good, respectful communication. It is about making sure you are discussing things openly, rather than simply arguing. It is about staying involved and appreciating differences and not withdrawing or avoiding conflict. The two most important communication skills are listening empathetically and speaking up respectfully. You want to understand the other person's point of view and help them understand yours as well. Remember these two skills form the building blocks of resolving disagreements and when applied over time can resolve even the most serious conflict.

Tips for the Future

When you next find yourself in a dispute, practice:

1. Pausing rather than reacting
2. Active listening before you respond
3. Respectfully speaking up and giving your point of view.

STEP 6: EMPOWERING TEENAGERS

As mentioned earlier, parenting teenagers is a bit like teaching them to fly their own plane. During these years, the parent acts like a co-pilot, ready to teach and support the trainee pilot. Though it can be hard, you have to learn to relinquish the controls bit by bit and support your teenager as they learn to take responsibility. In addition, you have to remain sufficiently involved in your teenager's life, so that they seek out your support and accept your influence. In other words, you may have to work very hard to stay connected to your teenager so that they will allow you into the co-pilot's seat in the first place, and won't later push the ejector button and sack you from the role before the job is complete!

Just as the long-term aim of the co-pilot is to empower their trainees to become fully qualified pilots, so the long-term aim of the parent is to empower their teenagers to become confident, capable adults who are responsible for their own lives. However, this is harder than it seems and many parents fall into the trap of being 'disempowering' rather than 'empowering' parents.

Disempowering Parenting

Below are three styles of disempowering parenting which you can easily fall into, despite the best of intentions. However, each of these styles cultivates irresponsibility in teenagers and does not prepare them for the task of being an adult:

INDULGENT

Doing everything for your teenagers. For example, waking them in the morning, making their breakfast and lunch, tidying up for them, washing their clothes, covering for them when they miss homework etc.

CRITICAL

Nagging, correcting, instructing teenagers over every task without giving them space and responsibility. For example, nagging them to mow the lawn and then standing over them while they do it, even criticising their work.

PERMISSIVE

Giving your teenagers excessive space, so that you are uninvolved and have little influence in their lives (meaning they learn little from you).

Empowering Parenting

BE ENCOURAGING

Perhaps the most empowering thing you can do as a parent is to be supportive and encouraging. Begin to trust your teenagers and express your belief in their ability to succeed. Highlight and identify what they do right and the good qualities that they have. See yourself as a coach in their lives: you cheer them on when they are successful, provide a shoulder to cry on when they experience disappointment, and are there to chat to in the ordinary times. No matter what, you are always on their side. Even when they do wrong, you help them take responsibility; you aim to teach them, but you always support and encourage them. Perhaps the greatest gift we can give our children is to maintain an unwavering belief in them during bad times or periods of discouragement.

LET TEENAGERS TAKE RESPONSIBILITY FOR HOUSEHOLD AND FAMILY TASKS

This suggestion should be welcome relief to overburdened parents who do everything for their teenagers – you do them no service by taking charge of their lives in this way. It robs them of a chance to learn important life skills and to develop a sense of pride in carrying out jobs well. Doing everything for teenagers also disempowers them because it inadvertently communicates that they are not capable of carrying out the tasks themselves. During the teenage years you should handover household and family tasks to them one by one, so that they eventually take on fair adult responsibility in the running of a home. Michael and Terri Quinn have compiled the below list of all the tasks which parents could handover to teenagers. They recommend using it as a checklist to periodically review:

» Weekly household shopping
» Choosing their own clothes
» Getting up in the morning
» Washing-up
» Mowing the grass
» Painting a room
» Paying bills
» Locking doors at night
» Cooking meals
» Cleaning the house
» Washing clothes
» Doing basic repairs
» Ironing
» Changing the oil in the car
» Mending an electric fuse
» Wiring an electric plug
» Caring for a younger child
» Cleaning the windows
» Planting flowers and vegetables
» Leading prayers
» Chopping firewood
» Settling their own squabbles

TEACH TEENAGERS TO MAKE THEIR OWN DECISIONS

Teaching teenagers to make decisions about their own lives is the most important task that parents can hand over. Parents should empower teenagers to make decisions such as how to manage their routine, their choice of friends, their lifestyle, and planning for their future. Rather than giving ready-made answers to these questions, it's best if parents step back and support teenagers in deciding for themselves. For example, if your son approaches and asks you whether he should take French or history as an exam subject, it may be best for you not to give an immediate answer but to ask 'What do you think yourself?' 'What do you think are the pros and cons for each subject?' This way, you encourage your son to work out this decision for himself and prepare him for making decisions later in life. Stepping back and allowing teenagers to evaluate life choices and their consequences can be hard when you don't agree with some of their decisions. For example, it may be difficult to step back and listen first when your thirteen-year-old daughter wants to get her nose pierced or your fourteen-year-old son wants to know what you think of his crazy haircut.

TAKE TIME TO TEACH YOUR TEENAGER

You can't suddenly hand over responsibility to a teenager without first taking the time to teach and prepare them for it. We often assume teenagers know how to do basic chores, even when no one has taught them. Just because they have watched you do the laundry or the ironing for many years doesn't mean they have learnt how to do it themselves. It takes skill, tact and time to teach someone something in a way that empowers and motivates them. This is the difference between nagging a child to mow the lawn, which they might do badly, and teaching them an appreciation of gardening over time, so that they take pride in the result. In preparing children to take responsibility for a task it can be helpful to take time to:

1. Explain clearly what has to be done. Give them an appreciation of the purpose of the task.
2. Ask them what help they will need from you in order to learn the task. For example, you can demonstrate what has to be done, you can do the task together, or you can let them go off and do the task and come back to you to report progress; or you can do all three in sequence.
3. As far as possible, let them make choices about how the task is done. For example, you don't mind when your daughter does her ironing and washing, just that it is not in the living room. For some tasks you can encourage your teenager to be creative. For example, on your son's night to cook, you can let him surprise you with the menu.
4. Make your teenager accountable for the task, getting credit if it is done and experiencing consequences if not.

ALLOW TEENAGERS TO LEARN FROM CONSEQUENCES

Responsibility means experiencing the good and bad consequences of our actions. Just as it is important to let teenagers take credit for achievements and take pride in a job well done, it is also important to let them experience what happens when things go wrong so they can learn from their mistakes. Parents can often rescue teenagers by covering for them when they don't do their homework, by giving them pocket money even though they did not complete the expected chore, or by ironing their shirt at the last minute even though they can do it themselves. Letting teenagers experience consequences and learn from mistakes is not abandoning them, rather it is teaching them to take responsibility for their actions.

Even in doing this, you can still be encouraging and on their side, helping them learn, but you are not there to take over and rescue them. Consider the following example:

> *Thirteen-year-old Joe wanted to leave the football team. He didn't really enjoy it and wanted out. Bob, his father, was worried. Joe didn't do much other physical activity and didn't have many friends. He was worried his son would be moping around the house bored all summer. He listened to Joe and expressed his concerns, but Joe was adamant that he wanted to leave. In the end, Bob did not object but supported Joe in making his own decision. Sure enough, during the summer Joe began to complain that he was bored, that he had nothing to do and no friends to hang out with. Bob didn't react righteously with an 'I told you so' (though he felt like it), instead he bit his lip and empathised with how Joe was feeling. Being listened to, Joe was able to admit that he 'sort of regretted' leaving football, though he still wanted to do something different. Bob told him that it took courage to face regrets and he asked Joe would he like some help in thinking what to do next. Joe readily agreed and together they found a different sports club, which Joe made a commitment to attend.*

MAKE TEACHING FUN

Teaching a teenager a new task does not have to be boring and formal. The more fun and enjoyable you make it, the better. For example, you can ask your son to do a six-week cookery course with you; or offer to decorate your daughter's room with her and use the time to teach her painting skills; or you can suggest a family spring cleaning day (followed by a big family treat), when each teenager chooses a special task but when you all work together. Such shared activities are often times of great connection between parents and children.

START SMALL

Becoming an empowering parent can mean a big transition. If you are a parent who does everything for your teenagers it can be difficult to suddenly relinquish all your jobs, and your teenagers would doubtless not be prepared to take them on. It is best to start by picking out something small that you are going to teach your teenagers to do. Perhaps you are not going to wash up every evening, instead asking your children to do a night each, or you're not going to take responsibility for getting them up every morning, or for doing their laundry. Whatever you decide, it's best to sit down in advance to talk about letting them take some responsibility for household chores and family tasks, explaining the benefits of this. Listen to their ideas and views (you may be surprised that they are very reasonable) and explain your own ideas. When you do start this new approach, expect some resistance and teething problems. Teenagers may agree to do tasks but find it hard to follow through and take responsibility. In addition, they are bound to test your word and you have to keep your part of the bargain. They need to discover that if they don't do their own laundry then nobody will magically step in and they really will have nothing to wear on Saturday night!

Tips for the Future

1. Pick a family task or household chore you want to hand over to your teenagers.
2. Sit down and talk to them; explain why you want to hand it over to them (e.g. a fairer system, teaching them responsibility).
3. Agree to teach them the task if needed.
4. Agree on the rewards of doing the task and the consequences of not completing it.
5. Arrange to review how they got on.

STEP 7: NEGOTIATING RULES AND BOUNDARIES

One evening, fifteen-year-old Paul tells his parents that he wants to stay over at his friend Bill's house the forthcoming Halloween night. His parents, who have only met Bill twice, are unsure, and they tell Paul they want to speak to Bill's parents first. Paul doesn't want this, saying it would be 'humiliating'. He wants his parents to trust him instead.

What decisions should teenagers make for themselves and what rules and boundaries should parents establish? What are reasonable rules to set for teenagers and how do you enforce them in a way that teaches self-responsibility?

This section gives some suggestions as to how parents might negotiate and establish rules with their teenagers, a process which, when handled correctly, can teach a young person responsibility and build mutual respect between parent and child. We build on all the valuable skills already covered (such as pressing the pause button, listening during conflict and speaking up assertively).

Remember the 'Big Picture'

Parenting is a long-term task. The goal is to help teenagers learn how to be responsible adults who confidently make their own decisions. Rules should be seen as a flexible set of guidelines and agreements which are established to help navigate this long parenting journey. Good rules allow children to take responsibility for their actions and to learn from their mistakes. You don't want a set of rules that over-controls a young person, meaning that they never learn for themselves. Nor do you want no rules or boundaries at all, where a young person is exposed to unnecessary risk and has few guidelines to learn from. You want rules that protect young people, but that also let them learn to take more responsibility for themselves.

INVOLVE YOUNG PEOPLE IN DECIDING FAMILY RULES

Negotiate, negotiate and negotiate. These are the three most important principles in agreeing rules with teenagers. The more they are involved in the discussion, the more you listen to them; and the more you try and accommodate their views and wishes, the more likely they are to respect and uphold the rules. The process of negotiation can take time. It involves lots of discussions, lots of one-to-ones and possibly lots of family meetings. Busy parents can often be tempted simply to impose a rule or make a quick decision. However, this overlooks the benefits of negotiation. The process of negotiation ensures that you as a parent remain appropriately involved in your teenagers' lives. It gives you a chance to connect with them and to communicate your own values and feelings. In addition, it teaches young people how to express themselves and to think through their own opinions and values. It is certainly worth the time.

Rules work best when they are family agreements that everyone was involved in creating and that everyone tries to keep. For example, if you're concerned as a parent about the amount of TV your kids watch, rather than simply imposing a rule such as 'No TV before 6 p.m.', why not spend some time (perhaps in a family meeting – see Step 9) discussing the issue, highlighting the benefits and drawbacks of TV, and trying to come to an agreement. Remember, this could take time and lots of listening (and several meetings!), but if you arrive at an agreement you have achieved a priceless goal in teaching responsibility.

KEEP 'NON-NEGOTIABLE' RULES TO A MINIMUM

Parents often make the mistake of having too many rules for their teenagers, which can lead to conflict and rob teenagers of the chance to make their own decisions. For example, do you really have to insist your daughter tidies her room to your standards, or can you close the door and let her take responsibility? Or you may not like your son's haircut, but maybe it's best not to make an issue out of it and let him decide how to wear his hair. While there are times when you have to make rules that your teenager might not agree with, these should be kept to a minimum and reserved to really important things such as safety, education and health. It helps to think in advance about which rules are really important to you as a parent. Often families sit down and come up with these together. 'Non-negotiable' rules might include:

» No drug taking
» Letting you know where they are
» Not travelling alone at night
» Friends welcome in the house, but only when an adult is at home.

Even when you do make a rule that your teenager doesn't like, it is still important to talk it through with them and to listen to their point of view and feelings. In addition, teenagers might find it easier to accept a rule when they are given choices about how it is enforced. In the example at the beginning of this chapter, the father could help fifteen-year-old Paul accept the rule by giving the following choice:

I'm sorry Paul, but if you want to stay over at your friend Bill's house then I want to ring his parents first to check it's okay. I understand that you find this a bit embarrassing but I need to know you will be safe. You may want to tell his parents first that I'm going to ring if that is easier for you – that's your choice – but I need to talk to them before you go.

SHOW HOW RULES BENEFIT YOUR TEENAGER

In discussing rules with teenagers it helps to explain to them how they can benefit and how you are only setting them out of care and concern for them. For example, you can tell your teen that you are only insisting that he studies as you want him to do his best in school and don't want him to miss out on any opportunities. Or you can reason with your daughter that you would not be a good parent if you did not collect her after a night out; that as a parent it is your job to ensure she is safe.

You can also turn the tables and ask your teenager, 'What would you do if you were the parent?' Though you might think they may give a permissive answer, often teenagers can begin to see your perspective. Once teenagers understand that the rules are for their benefit and set out of concern and love for them, it helps a lot in gaining their cooperation.

The Important Rule of Respect

Respect is one of the most important rules of all. You have to insist that your teenagers speak and act respectfully towards you and others, just as you have to observe this rule yourself in communicating with them. It is often this rule that causes the most problems. Many parents complain about their teenagers' lack of respect, attitude or tantrums. It is these behaviours that cause the most stress and unhappiness in families. However, this is the rule that is often least insisted upon. Parents may work hard to insist their teen gets to school, but put up with shouting and abuse from them. In addition, parents most frequently break this rule themselves and end up shouting or being disrespectful in return. By doing so, you lose your authority as a parent.

The centrality of respect is of utmost importance, and so it is always recommended that you 'pause' negative exchanges and insist on this rule being kept. For example: 'John, you are shouting, I can only talk to you when you speak politely' or 'I am getting too angry now, we'll take a break and talk later.' By modelling this self-control and implementing the rule of respect, you teach your teenagers a valuable lesson. Children learn more from how you behave than what you ask of them.

Establishing Routines

Establishing routines is the key to a happy household. Rather than having an ongoing battle with your daughter about how long she spends on Facebook, setting clear rules about time spent online can establish a habit and thus avoid ongoing conflict. There are many different routines that can be helpful to establish, such as:

1. Evening and bedtime (e.g. technology off at a certain time, and in bed at a certain hour)
2. Homework (e.g. homework done before going out or going online)
3. Mealtimes (e.g. all family sit down for dinner at 6 p.m.)
4. Weekly chores (e.g. each person is on a rota that is agreed each week).

The key to establishing routines is to first decide what you want and to be very clear about what the ideal routine might be. You then need to negotiate this with your teenagers, in order to incorporate their needs and wishes. Good routines should be clear and specific and broken down into steps. Sometimes it can help to write them on a chart that makes it clear for everyone.

ENCOURAGING TEENS TO KEEP RULES AND ROUTINES
Starting a new routine can be hard work, especially if it is different to what has gone before. For example, if you are establishing a new routine that disallows technology, such as phones or computers, during mealtimes or after 10 p.m., this might be hard for teenagers to get used to (as well as for parents, who may also be attached to technology).

Sometimes it is useful to offer an incentive to reward teenagers for their hard work, particularly in the early days before it becomes a habit. For example, you might give teenagers some extra pocket money if they do their weekly chore, or arrange a special family outing if everyone keeps the rule of no technology at mealtimes. Even if you don't use tangible rewards, it is important to be very encouraging towards teenagers as they learn to keep new rules. For example, 'Look, I know it is hard, but once you get started it will be easier' and 'I appreciate you doing this, it means a lot to me.'

Tips for the Future

1. Make a list of the really important rules you want kept in your house (this can be a great exercise to do with the whole family).
2. Negotiate the exact form of these rules with your teenagers and ask what they consider to be the most important rules in the home.
3. Think through the key routines in the household (e.g. morning and the school run, homework and mealtimes, weekly chores) and mark them on a chart with your teenagers. It can be a good idea to assess how they are working as part of a weekly family meeting (see Step 9).

STEP 8: FOLLOWING THROUGH ON RULES

My fifteen-year-old son pays no attention to me when I ask him to do something. I am always nagging him to get off the computer and to clean his room but he just ignores me or says he will do it but doesn't in the end. I find myself losing the head with him over it.

You won't be surprised to hear that even though you can reach agreements about rules with your teenagers, they can still break them or refuse to cooperate later. You might ask your teenager politely and assertively to do something and they will still say no. The route to teenagers taking responsibility involves lots of challenging and testing of limits. Once you encounter resistance or rule breaking, the temptation might be to revert to shouting at or cajoling your teenager to behave. However, these strategies can be ineffective and also damage your relationship with your teenager over time.

Instead, it is recommended that you remain in control of the situation by offering your teen the choice to behave or to experience the consequences of their actions. Consequences provide you with a clear enforceable plan of action for what to do if you encounter resistance and rule breaking, and teaches young people to behave in the long term.

Agreeing on Consequences

Consequences work best if they are reasonable and fair, and if the teenager has been involved in deciding them. Discussing consequences with teenagers in advance gains their cooperation and treats them as accountable adults. Ask your teenagers what they think the fair consequence to breaking a rule or an agreement should be. You may be surprised that they will generate better and more effective examples than you thought of yourself! For example:

» If Rob is an hour late coming in, then he has to be in an hour earlier the next night.

» If Sue does not do her chores for the week, either she has to do double chores the next week or she doesn't get her pocket money.
» If James does not arrive home for a family dinner, no cooked meal will be available for him.
» If Orla does not get up early enough, she has to walk to school without a lift.
» If Peter does not do his washing and ironing, he will have no clean clothes on Saturday.

If the agreement is not working then it should be discussed again, rather than forgotten about. For example, if the washing-up rota is not being followed, you should discuss it again at the next family meeting (see Step 9). Knowing that there is a review time, when they will be accountable to other family members, is a powerful motivating factor for teenagers to 'get their act together' and to do what they promised.

Making Consequences Work

REMIND TEENAGERS OF THE BEHAVIOUR YOU EXPECT

Prior to enforcing a consequence, make sure that the teenager is reminded about the behaviour you expect. For example, 'John, I want you to turn off the computer and start your homework as agreed.' Even when you offer a choice, the key is to make sure you keep the focus on the expected outcome. So, rather than saying, 'If you don't do your homework now, you will not be allowed on the computer at all', it is more effective to say, 'Come on, get your homework started and you will have more computer time later.'

CONSEQUENCES ONLY HAVE TO BE SMALL TO WORK

Insisting your teen is grounded for ten minutes can be as effective as the whole day. Also this means the consequence is over quickly, giving the teenager a chance to behave well again. It also means that you have further options and can reapply the consequence later if needed (e.g. grounding the teen for a further ten minutes).

ENSURE CONSEQUENCES AFFECT THE TEEN AND NOT YOU

A mistake that parents make is to propose a consequence that affects them more than the teenager. For example, you might say, 'If you don't behave, we will cancel the visit to Granny.' But of course you also want to visit Granny! By using this consequence you punish yourself and not the teen.

PLAN CONSEQUENCES IN ADVANCE

It is hard to think of consequences when you are under pressure and feeling upset and annoyed. Under these conditions you are likely to pick a consequence that is too severe, too hard to carry out, or one that simply will not work. For this reason, it is really important to plan consequences in advance of situations arising. Sit down and think what consequences are best for your teen in each likely situation.

ALWAYS BE RESPECTFUL

Choices and consequences work best when you are respectful and calm, encouraging even. For example, 'C'mon John, I don't want to have take away any more of your pocket money, so calm down now and behave.'

ENFORCE CONSEQUENCES CALMLY

The essential thing about enforcing consequences is that it is a time for *action* and not *words*. It is best if a parent follows through calmly and firmly with the consequence without reasoning or scolding. Things can be talked about at another time.

NEVER RUN OUT OF CONSEQUENCES

Always have an extra consequence up your sleeve. Think through what you will do if your teen does not behave after the first consequence. Make your consequences small enough so you never run out. For example, instead of stopping them from watching an entire TV programme, why not just ten or even five minutes of it? This means you can repeat the consequence by docking the teen another five minutes if they don't respond to the initial consequence.

Setting Up Planned Consequences

As just suggested, it can be useful to establish a system of planned consequences with teenagers that you can use in most situations. To do this, you need to identify a privilege that is small and repeatable and which you can use frequently and daily without running out. TV/computer time and pocket money are two good examples, with pocket money being the most versatile. A possible pocket money sanction system might look like this:

1. Decide on the daily amount of pocket money you will give your teenager. Try and make this correspond to what they get from you normally. For example, if they get €14 a week, then the daily amount is €2.

2. Decide on how many sanctions you are likely to need on your worst day and divide the money accordingly. For example, if you feel your son could misbehave four times a day then the sanction amount should be 50 cent.

3. Explain the system to your children in advance. Be positive about the purpose, which might be to help them get on together, or to learn better ways of resolving disagreements.

4. Allocate the money at the end of day and start afresh the following day with a new amount; e.g. at a chosen time, give your son the pocket money saying something like, 'You earned €1.50 today, you lost money for shouting and being rude, but you still got €1.50. I hope you will get the full amount tomorrow.'

Following Through on Consequences

Following through is about you, as a parent, keeping the promises and agreements you have made with your teenagers, so that they learn to do likewise. It is about not giving in and ironing your son's shirt for him at the last minute because you feel sorry for him, or taking your daughter to school in the car when you agreed before that she should take responsibility for what time she gets up. Keeping these promises can be hard on parents, which makes it important only to set consequences which you know you can keep yourself.

It is best not to make a fuss about it or use it as an opportunity to lecture your teenager by saying, for example, 'I knew you would not be able to get up on time. This is typical.' Instead, try and be calm, firm and matter-of-fact. You can even be supportive but do not rescue. For example, it is okay to say when your son misses an agreed family meal, 'I'm sorry you're hungry', but it would be a mistake to make him a special meal.

In addition, if you agree that a rule (e.g. a chore rota) will be reviewed later at a family meeting, it is important that this meeting takes place and that you don't avoid the discussion for fear of upsetting your teenager or inviting trouble. By keeping your side of the bargain, you model responsibility and make teenagers accountable for their actions.

Consequences for Serious Problems

Even with serious problems, establishing consequences with teenagers can help them take responsibility for their actions. Often these consequences can be presented as choices. For example:

Parent: I can't stand by and let you use drugs with your friends. I'm too concerned about you. Either you choose to stop or you come with me to see the drugs counsellor.

Parent: If you get suspended from school then you must stay in and study for the period you are suspended. You won't be allowed out or to play computer games.

In dealing with serious problems, consequences aren't a 'magic solution' but they can play a useful role in helping a teen take responsibility, in addition to many other positive parenting techniques such as listening, encouraging and problem solving together.

Tips for the Future

1. Review the list of important family rules you made after Step 7.
2. Now make a list of possible consequences if these rules are not kept.
3. Make a plan as to how you might follow through on each of the consequences.
4. Consider how you will explain these consequences to your teenagers and get them to accept them.

STEP 9: SOLVING PROBLEMS AND TALKING THINGS THROUGH

The secret to getting along with your teenagers and reducing conflict is finding better ways of communicating with them – ways to listen and to get through to them. While this is true of all children, it is especially true of teenagers who are developing more of an adult relationship with their parents. Most of the ideas in this book have been geared towards improving communication within families. Good communication is the basis for solving problems. Connecting with teenagers, finding out about their world and listening and speaking to them in the good times provide a solid basis for solving problems during the rough times.

Family Meetings

One way that families can stay connected and keep the lines of communication open is to organise regular family meetings. These can be used to talk together about important issues, make plans (such as for holidays) and negotiate family rules (such as how much TV is allowed, or who does the washing up). Meetings run best when they are democratic, with a special emphasis on trying to reach consensus or win-win agreements. Though parents might initially lead, it can help to alternate the role of chair. Give someone else the responsibility of writing down decisions, and another person that of keeping track of time.

Once family meetings become established they can have a transforming effect. Many parents describe them as invaluable in altering the tone of family life from conflict and distance to cooperation and closeness. Family meetings provide a routine way for parents to stay connected with their children, to listen to their concerns and share their own views. However, parents also report that family meetings can be difficult to establish, especially with teenagers who are initially suspicious or cynical about the process. Drawing a teenager into participating can take time but it is well worth the effort.

DRAWING TEENAGERS INTO FAMILY MEETINGS

1. Introduce the meeting as important but informal:
   Rather than making the meeting sound formal, it can be helpful to introduce them in an informal way. For example, 'I thought it would be a good idea if we could all have a meal together every Thursday. It would also give us time afterwards to discuss the summer holidays. I want to hear your views on where we should go.'

2. Make meetings relevant to their concerns:
   Make sure the meetings address issues that matter to your teenager, as well as issues that matter to you. For example, if your daughter says she feels lumbered with all the household chores, or your son approaches you saying he wants a TV in his room, rather than solving these disputes there and then, say, 'Why don't you bring it up at the next family meeting?' If these are issues that they feel strongly about they are likely to attend and participate.

3. Share power during the meeting:
   Attending family meetings is usually attractive to teenagers once they see that it is a forum where they will get a fair hearing and can have an input in how family decisions are made. For this reason, share power in the meetings – encourage teenagers to fill the role of chair or note taker from time to time. In addition, go slow during meetings. Decisions can be postponed until the next meeting if there is not enough time. The main focus is on listening and understanding, making sure everyone has a chance to air their views.

4. Make meetings fun:
   A lot of families end their meeting with a game or a special group activity. Teens can take turns in selecting the activities.

5. Don't make meetings compulsory:
   Don't get into a power struggle, forcing a teenager to attend a family meeting, as this can defeat the purpose. Instead, strongly encourage them to attend, making it attractive for them to do so. Let them experience the consequences if they don't attend, for example, not being there when important decisions affecting them are made, missing out on a favourite meal and a fun time.

Persist:

Don't worry if teenagers come with an attitude or appear uninterested from time to time; this is quite normal. Instead, persist with respectful communication on your part. Even the most 'switched off' teenager can eventually open up and participate.

Solving Problems

The mark of a healthy family is not whether they have problems or not, but how they go about trying to solve them. What counts is being able to sit down and talk through problems as they arise. Once a family is able to do this, they can get through most of the difficult times. Below is a six-stage model you can use to solve problems. This model can be used during a family meeting when everyone is present, with an individual or with your partner when you have a difference of opinion, or even by yourself to think through a dilemma you have. The six stages are:

1. Connecting and setting time and space aside
2. Listening first
3. Speaking up respectfully
4. Thinking up solutions
5. Choosing the best solutions and making agreements
6. Meeting again and following up.

The first three stages have already been covered in earlier steps, and indeed these basic skills of connecting with teenagers, listening first and speaking up with respect are often sufficient in themselves to solve problems. This is especially true in the case of listening. The source of most conflict between parents and teenagers is misunderstanding and a lack of trust. Once this is resolved through empathetic listening, much of the conflict dissolves and solutions can flow naturally. Stages 4 to 6 describe how solutions and agreements can be established.

THINKING UP SOLUTIONS

Once you have understood your teenager's point of view and expressed your own feelings, you are in a position to brainstorm possible solutions to the problems you are facing together. Rather than simply giving your own solutions, it is important to hold back and first encourage your teenager to come up with ideas and ways forward. Ask questions such as, 'How do you think you can solve this?', 'How can you ensure you get home on time?', 'How can you convince the teachers that you're trying a little harder?' Though it's tempting to come up with your own answers, it is crucial to proceed at the teenager's pace and to wait for them to suggest solutions. Solutions generated by teenagers are far more likely to be carried through by them. You will be surprised at how even the most difficult teenager, when given time, can come up with solutions which are as good as or even better than those thought up by parents. Parents can add their own ideas and suggestions, but this is best done after your teenager's ideas have been explored or when they specifically ask you for suggestions.

At the brainstorming stage it is important to generate as many alternative solutions as possible – the more you have the better. It is also important not to be critical at this stage. Encourage your teenager's creativity and listen to all the ideas they come up with. These can include solutions tried successfully in the past. You can help your teenager recall times when things were going better or the problem was solved. For example, you can ask, 'How have you solved this in the past?' or 'Do you remember last year we had the same problem, but we got through it? How did we do that then?' Once talked about and understood, these past solutions are more easily repeated.

CHOOSING THE BEST SOLUTIONS AND MAKING AGREEMENTS

Now it is time to help your teenager decide which solutions they are going to use. During this stage the emphasis is on helping teenagers think through the consequences of the ideas suggested at the brainstorming stage, in order to identify those which will have the best results both for them and other people. Frequently teenagers come up with unrealistic or inappropriate solutions. However, rather than criticising you can guide them by asking them to think of the consequences. Asking questions like, 'What do you think will happen if you try that?' can be helpful. For example, as a way of avoiding a bully, a teenager might suggest dropping out of the school team. Yet on thinking it through, he might realise that he would miss being part of the club. With the support of his parent he may come up with a different solution, such as confronting the bully or gaining the support of the other boys to do something about it.

MEETING AGAIN AND FOLLOWING UP

When the best solution is chosen, it is important to arrange a time to review how things are going. This is a crucial and often forgotten stage. Solving problems takes time and sometimes persistence is needed to make a breakthrough. If an attempted solution doesn't work out it is important to meet again to find out what happened and to support your teenager in finding a new course of action. Even if things do work out, meeting again gives you a chance to encourage and compliment your teenager, thus empowering them. In addition, by following up on agreements, you make your teenagers (and yourself) accountable and encourage them to take responsibility for their actions.

Problem Solving in Action

Let's look at this problem-solving model at work. We will continue the example introduced in Step 5, in which fifteen-year-old Lisa is discussing leaving school with her father, Bill. After initially flying off the handle, Bill pressed the pause button and set aside a time to talk to his daughter calmly. First he listened to her describe her struggles in school, and then expressed his concerns about her leaving early. In the dialogue below they go on to look at possible solutions:

BRAINSTORMING AND THINKING UP SOLUTIONS

Bill: Mightn't you be able to turn things around at school?
Lisa: I don't know.
Bill: Well, what would help?
Lisa: Well it's mainly Irish and history that I get into trouble in.

Bill: Maybe we could look at getting you extra help for those classes.

Lisa: Or maybe I could get out of doing them altogether, and just concentrate on the others.

Bill: Maybe, we'd have to talk to the head about that. What could you do to help?

Lisa: Well, I could try and keep out of trouble and work harder.

Bill: That might help.

Lisa: I also still wonder if I would be better leaving and getting an apprenticeship somewhere.

Bill: That is another possibility.

Lisa: Or if I did leave, maybe I could study at home and still do the exams?

Bill: Possibly.

Notice how at this crucial stage Bill is encouraging Lisa to come up with solutions herself. He does not criticise her ideas but encourages her to identify as many potential solutions as possible. The aim at this stage of problem solving is to be creative and to work with your teenager to generate lots of ideas and possibilities.

CHOOSING THE BEST SOLUTIONS

Bill: So we've got a few ideas then. We could try and get you extra help for the classes or talk to the principal about reducing the time you spend in some classes. And you could think of how to keep out of trouble and work a bit harder. Or you could look at leaving school at some stage and either seeking a job, or maybe doing the exams while at home. What do you think?

Lisa: I'll try and give it another go at school, maybe we could talk to the principal, but I'm not sure it will work

Bill: We can still look at the other options. It's probably a good idea that you look at what you want to do when you leave school anyway – sooner or later. It would be good if you could leave with some exams.

REVIEWING HOW YOU GET ON

Bill: How does that sound?

Lisa: Okay.

Bill: We'll talk about it again next week.

Though problem solving may take a lot longer in real life, especially for a difficult issue (and that is why it is crucial for Bill to meet Lisa to talk again), the above example illustrates the different steps you can take to talk through problems with young people.

Tips for the Future

1. Set aside a time to talk through a problem with your teenager using the six-stage model described in this chapter.
2. Rather than immediately giving solutions, remember to hold back and to help them generate their own solutions. Listen to their ideas first and add yours later.
3. Make sure to agree a plan for how you will proceed and make a time in the future to review how you get on.

STEP 10: PARENTS CARING FOR THEMSELVES

There was a man working furiously in the woods trying to saw down a tree. He was making very little progress, as his saw was blunt and becoming blunter with each stroke. The man was hot and frustrated and continued to work harder and harder. A friend noticed what was going on and asked him, 'Why don't you stop for a few minutes so you can sharpen your saw?'

'Don't you see,' replied the man, 'I'm too busy sawing to take any time off.'

Stephen Covey uses the above story to illustrate the futility of working non-stop and the importance of parents taking time off to renew themselves. So many parents become martyrs to their children, devoting all their time and energy to the task of parenting without thinking of their own needs and wishes. Other parents become excessively focused on the problems and conflicts they have with their children, and all their energy is spent on disagreeing, correcting and rowing with them. In both positions not only is the parent liable to burn out from stress and exhaustion, but their parenting becomes increasingly counterproductive and negative. By becoming a martyr, the parent can become resentful and/or run down, with little energy to relate to their children in a consistent loving way. While the correcting approach is liable to increase the power struggle between parent and teenager, leading to further rebellion until either the parent gives up or the teen walks out.

As the story above suggests, it is crucial to take time out to 'sharpen the saw'. Parents should press the pause button and take time to look after their own needs, as well as attending to the needs of their children. When parents' own need for care, comfort and fulfilment are met, they are freed up to attend fully to the parenting role. Children need cared-for parents as much as they need parents to care for them. The best way to help your teens grow into confident adults with high self-esteem is for you to model this – that is, to take steps to value, love and prioritise yourself.

You may protest that you simply can't afford to take time out for yourself. The reality is that you can't afford not to. Think about the times you have been run down or exhausted and how it was impossible to do any of the 'more important' tasks. Remember the times you felt energetic and good about yourself and how easy it was then to achieve things and to be kind and loving to others. A little bit of self-care goes a long way.

HOW TO SHARPEN THE SAW

Self-care and personal renewal are basically about achieving balance in your life. It is about trying to ensure you address your different needs in a balanced way. There are four dimensions of self-care and personal renewal, which we need to address frequently in order to have a balanced and stress-free life:

1. Physical: exercise (such as walking, jogging, playing sports); eating well and healthily; getting good rest and relaxation.
2. Mental: keeping your mind stimulated with other interests (such as reading, movies, theatre etc.); learning new things.
3. Emotional: keeping in contact with friends; connecting with family (e.g. having a special night out with your partner); doing self-nurturing things (e.g. treating yourself to a special bath or a shopping trip).
4. Spiritual: time alone for personal reflection; meditating/prayer; goal setting; reconnecting to your values.

The aim of self-care is look after your greatest asset in creating a happy family life – you. All the ideas in this book can only work with a vibrant, motivated and cared-for parent to implement them. Caring for yourself as a parent is crucial in making a difference to your relationship with your teenager and all the other steps depend upon it.

FAMILY RENEWAL

Taking time out to 'sharpen the saw' is something that applies equally well to family life. Healthy families find time to recharge themselves.

Much of what has been described in this book is about renewing and rebuilding family relationships; for example, connecting and sharing with family members, spending quality time with one another, listening empathetically and expressing our own feelings. All these activities 'sharpen the saw' for individual family members and for the family as a whole. Ensuring you have regular quality time – by yourself, with your partner, with your children and with your family as a whole – can be a way of not only eliminating stress but also finding personal meaning.

Tips for the Future

1. Set aside a special time, just for yourself, doing something you really enjoy.
2. Plan to spend relaxing time with your partner away from problems. If you are a single parent, do the same with a close friend or other family member.

PART 2
Common Teenage Problems and Issues

EDUCATION, SCHOOL AND MOTIVATION

My thirteen-year-old son has lost interest in school

Q. *My thirteen-year-old son has never really applied himself in school, particularly in the last year. As a result, it can be a battle to get him to sit down and do homework, and we seem to be always in conflict about this. Recently, he has started saying that he is not interested in school and that he wants to do other things. I'm wondering what to do, whether I should just take the pressure off and let him do badly in school and not reach his potential. Or is there something else I could do to encourage him. For example, can you bribe/incentivise adolescent boys in relation to homework? Could I pay him to do a bit more homework and is this a good idea?*

A. Parents have a responsibility to support their children's education and to set rules and routines around school and homework. Indeed, many studies show that when parents take a positive interest in their child's education by working closely with schools and supporting their children's learning at home, this leads to better educational outcomes for their children.

TAKE A POSITIVE APPROACH
However, it is crucial that this support is positive because if homework becomes a negative experience and a constant battle between parent and child, then this sort of parental attention can be counterproductive and can reinforce the child's negative view of education as well as damaging the parent-child relationship. You are right to take a step back and to consider if there are any other positive ways you can support your son's education and to help him reach his potential.

CHECK WHAT MAKES STUDY DIFFICULT FOR HIM
The first thing to do is really tune into your son and to understand what underpins his reluctance about homework. For example, it could be that he is struggling a bit with the schoolwork. Many intelligent children have a specific learning disability (such as an undiagnosed language disorder

or dyslexia) that makes it difficult for them to succeed within the formal learning system in school. You might want to talk to his teachers to see if this might be the case, because the recognition of specific learning problems can be a relief to children and there are specific supports that can make a big difference to their learning as well as to their confidence and motivation.

TUNE INTO WHAT MOTIVATES YOUR SON

Alternatively, your son may simply not be motivated about the curriculum or he may be questioning the value of the subjects he is being taught. Often this is the case when children approach adolescence, when they naturally question the point of adult values, such as education or exams. In this situation, take time to explore the value of education with your son. Take time to understand what motivates him and to see how this can be linked to school work and study. What are his specific talents and passions? What subjects in school is he good at and which ones inspire his interest? What are his hopes for his career and his life? It is important to start this adult conversation with him, so he can begin to understand the rationale for study and to make sense of his choices. Ultimately, unless your son is persuaded that school work is linked to achieving his own dreams and passions, he is likely to remain unmotivated.

It also helps to be creative about how learning happens and to find a way that builds on his strengths (for example, project-based learning, reading books about special interests together and so on).

HELP YOUR TEENAGER ESTABLISH A GOOD STUDY ROUTINE

In addition, some children may not be succeeding in homework as they are employing poor study strategies or don't have a good study routine. In these instances, there is a lot you can do to help as a parent, and in the Parents Plus programmes we suggest three specific steps to helping children study:

1. First, you need to agree a study routine with him which sets aside a distraction-free time to study in the day followed by a natural reward. For example, after school he might take a short break, then do an hour's homework/study, before doing a leisure activity such as a sport.

2. Secondly, it helps if you are around when he is studying and take an interest in his homework as he does it, without getting over-involved. This might mean helping him plan his homework and what he will do first, then taking a step back and letting him get on with it. You might check in with him occasionally and review progress, but you must give him space to do the homework himself.

3. The final step is to have a period of review after the homework and to go over what he has done – asking him what he learned and what he thought about the homework. Getting to know your son's subjects and being encouraging and interested in a genuine way is likely to be helpful in keeping him motivated and focused.

USE INCENTIVES AND REWARDS

You ask in your question whether it is a good idea to incentivise children with a reward or bribe to complete their homework. In my experience, this can work really well and increase a teenager's motivation, though it is important how you set this up. For example, you could establish a contract with your son whereby he can earn a small amount of pocket money each day he completes his homework. In the contract, you can clearly agree the steps of a good study routine and specify a time when you will review homework and talk about it.

The key is to find a reward that motivates your son and that you are happy to give. For example, if you don't want to give an extra reward, you can make an existing privilege – such as TV or PlayStation time or an existing pocket money allowance – dependent on completing homework; or you can have your son work towards a bigger reward in the future, for example, twenty successful homework completions results in a special trip.

TAKE A LONG-TERM VIEW

In helping a young teenager succeed in education, you can only go so far as a parent. Ultimately, it is down to the child how much effort they put in and what they choose as valuable. However, what you can do as a parent is to establish a good learning environment and to make rewards in the home dependent on putting in effort at study. Tune into your child's natural abilities and realise that while for some children the formal learning environment of school is where they excel, this is not the case for everyone. The key is to find out what your children's natural talents, interests and abilities are – whether these are within the school system or not – and to help them explore these in all aspects of their life.

My fifteen-year-old daughter won't study or tidy her room

Q. *My fifteen-year-old daughter isn't studying or doing homework at all in this, her Junior Cert year. She's very disorganised, regularly leaves school books at home and refuses to clean her room. She gets very angry when I try to encourage her to study or clean, spends all her time on the mobile phone, and has no interest in sport, drama or the arts. She seems to have totally lost her way and has no focus. How should I approach her?*

A. Study and preparing for exams can be stressful for students and parents alike. This is particularly the case in the run up to the Junior and Leaving Certificates, when the pressure and worry starts to mount in many homes. Lack of study can become a focal point for conflict between parents and teenagers, and the pressure often brings to the fore long-standing issues such as resentment over not doing chores or not participating in family life and so on.

TAKE A POSITIVE INTEREST

While it is important that as a parent you take an interest in your daughter's school work and encourage her to study, there is only so much you can do and, ultimately, she has to learn the importance of education and to make these decisions for herself. However, it is unacceptable that she is disrespectful to you by being angry and by not negotiating with you in a reasonable way.

Many teenagers use anger as a way of 'getting parents off their back' or as a means of avoiding talking about a hard issue. However, as a parent you do have a responsibility to talk to her about her study and education, and you are right to expect her to talk to you respectfully in return.

EMPLOY A CARROT-AND-STICK APPROACH

What generally works best in motivating teenagers is a balance of the carrot-and-stick approach. You need to both positively reach out to your teenagers, encouraging and supporting them, but also to hold them accountable for their actions and to provide for consequences. The first step always is to open the lines of communication with your teenager and to talk about the issue at hand.

As a result, it is important to try to find a way to talk with your daughter about exams and study and about what is going on for her. When raising the subject, it is important to pick the right time to talk to her – when she is more likely to be open. For some teenagers it can be helpful to give them a choice, saying for example, 'There is something important I need to talk about with you. Would you like to chat now or later?' For others it is best to raise the subject casually when you are doing something together.

PERSIST IN RAISING THE SUBJECT

If she fobs you off or refuses to have the conversation or gets angry to divert you from the subject, then you need to gently but firmly persist. It might be best to back off in the short term and then to return to the conversation later, but the important thing is that you follow up with her and try to talk again. You could say something such as, 'I appreciate that you find it hard to talk about study, but we need to talk' or 'Things seem to be hard for you at the moment and I want to support you' or 'As a parent I have a responsibility to ensure you do your best in school.' If she refuses to engage, you have the option to use some consequences – 'Until we have a reasonable conversation about what is going on, then I won't support your mobile phone use' and so on. This might provoke some anger in return, which you can address in this way: 'If you don't calm down then you will lose something else.' It is important not to let her anger thwart you from raising the issue.

LISTEN CAREFULLY WHEN SHE TALKS

When she does start talking to you about what is going on for her, the key is to first listen and to try to understand things from her perspective. You might be stressed or worried about her lack of study, but think how she might be feeling. She might be very worried herself and is likely to be experiencing a crisis of confidence in her ability. Perhaps she feels she can't study because she doubts her abilities to pass or perhaps she has got out of the habit and she finds it really hard to get started. Or perhaps there are other stresses on her mind or other problems she is dealing with. The more you can understand things from her perspective, the easier it will be to negotiate a plan with her.

The only way that you can move forward is with your daughter deciding that she wants to make progress, and while the exams are very close, there are still a lot of positive steps she can take in her study. Also, as a parent there are a lot of different ways that you can support her, such as helping create a study routine in the house, reviewing her different subjects with her, helping her make a study plan, offering to support her with grinds or extra classes, giving her rewards and incentives (such as fewer chores but only when she starts to study) and ensuring consequences (making privileges such as phone time dependent on study effort).

The important thing is to focus on small steps that she is willing to take rather than necessarily expecting a big turnaround. Even if you don't agree a plan forward, having a conversation that shows her you are concerned and interested in her is progress. This is especially the case if such a conversation opens up the lines of communication between you and makes it possible for her to talk to you again.

PUT THINGS IN PERSPECTIVE

While study and exams are important, you need to put these in perspective. More important is your daughter's well-being and happiness, as well as you having a positive relationship with her. If you put too much pressure on her about the exams and let this become a defining conflict between you, then this may not only be counterproductive but you also risk driving her further away from you. Whatever happens it is important to keep reaching out to her and to keep your relationship as positive as possible.

Should I relax the rules as my son is studying for the Leaving Certificate?

Q. *My son is eighteen and in Leaving Certificate year. I vacillate between letting him self-manage his time and losing the plot. His room is a permanent mess: clothes stored on the floor for months until I succumb and tidy (he is meant to keep his room in order). It's the same mess on the table he uses to study. He is doing an art portfolio for submission later this month and his homework and study for other subjects is suffering from lack of time. Input on how to manage the chaotic situation would be greatly appreciated, or do I just grin and bear it until June? My son is an only child and headstrong like myself.*

A. Your dilemma is a common one for parents of Junior and Leaving Cert students. It is difficult to know whether to let them off from normal household chores so they can have more time to study. Some parents argue that you should not make any allowances and that it is important to keep the routine as normal as possible. Indeed, there are potential benefits for teenagers continuing to do chores, as this can represent a helpful break from an intense study routine. In addition, for many teenagers taking responsibility to keep their desk or study space tidy can really assist their study plans and keep them focused and effective.

However, many parents argue the opposite, believing that it is important to make allowances and to reduce household chores in order to keep their teenager focused on studying. They feel that if he or she was distracted by cleaning up or doing chores, they would study less or that it would become a conflict that would interrupt the study schedule.

TUNE INTO YOUR TEENAGER

A lot depends on your teenager and what motivates and works best for them. Of course, if you do want to support him by making allowances and reducing chores, be careful of going too far and finding yourself putting up with unreasonable demands and behaviour. I have worked with some families who are tip-toeing around a grumpy, uncooperative teenager whose constant excuse is that they are studying. Teenagers are at a stage of life when they are challenging boundaries, so it is normal for them at times to push it with you or to try to get away with things. You have to be ready for this and to hold your ground on important matters.

TUNE INTO WHAT IS IMPORTANT TO YOU AS THE PARENT

In deciding how to respond, the first step is to think about what your teenager needs and also to be self-aware about what matters for you. Many parents are happy to pick up after their teenager and see this as a way of supporting them, particularly during the exam years. However, for other parents, this would lead to a great deal of resentment and anger.

Sometimes, it is a matter of degree. For example, as a parent you might be happy to relax the rule about his room being tidy, but find it important to keep the dining room table clear as this is a shared space.

NEGOTIATE WITH HIM ABOUT THE RULES

Whatever you decide, the next step is finding a positive way of communicating with your son and then negotiating a routine that works for you both – and for the rest of the family.

Pick a good time to talk things through with him. You can start by saying how you want to support him in his studying, but that as a family you also need to find a way to get all the chores done and to keep the place tidy. Ask him what his feelings are on the matter and how he thinks it can be resolved. You might be able to achieve some win-win solutions such as finding a different way of organising his study space, or you might try to negotiate some compromises. For example, you might agree to not notice his untidy room if he works harder at keeping the table he uses for study clear. You might be able to strike a deal with him that motivates him. To this end, you might say that you are prepared to tidy his room/let him off other chores as you want to support his study, but in return he needs to show you that he is working hard or doing his best.

TAKE AN INTEREST IN HIS STUDY

Finally, as a parent it can really help to take a interest in his study plans and routines. While you may not know the exact content of all the subjects he is learning, it does help if you take a interest in how he is approaching the study, what he is learning, what he is finding challenging, and so on. Providing a listening ear can be a real help to keeping a teenager motivated. In addition, many teenagers do need help with study skills, particularly in terms of how to plan and get started, how to structure the work, as well as how to make sure they implement plenty of breaks and balance study with rest and leisure. Being involved and supportive in this way can not only be helpful, but also allow you to feel close to him as you help him through this important milestone in his life.

PEER GROUP AND FRIENDSHIP PROBLEMS

Dealing with Bullying

Bullying can be a serious problem for children and teenagers and is, unfortunately, not uncommon. In some surveys up to 40 per cent of children report experiencing or being involved in bullying in school. Most tragic is that many children who are targeted are already marginalised or struggling in school, and up to half of all children who experience bullying suffer in silence and don't tell their parents or teachers what is going on. Bullying behaviours can be both physical and direct (such as slagging, intimidation and aggression) or more subtle and relational (such as exclusion, talking negatively about an individual to others or the silent treatment). Unfortunately, the growth of social media and texting has provided new avenues for bullying to take place, and given the public nature of these forums such bullying can be more devastating to children and teenagers. Bullying is also a complex group phenomenon that is reinforced by an audience and supported by the silence of bystanders. Many children who engage in bullying are not aware of its impact on the victim or may have also being victims of bullying themselves. As a result, all cases of bullying require a sensitive, thoughtful response.

HOW CAN YOU TELL IF YOUR CHILD IS BEING BULLIED?
Though some children are reluctant to tell if they are being bullied and keep it a secret, there are many indicators that your child might be being bullied or that they are coping with some other problem:

- » Sudden lack of confidence
- » Anxiety about going to school
- » Unexplained cuts or bruises
- » Poor school performance
- » Privacy about online communications

WHAT CAN YOU DO IF YOU SUSPECT YOUR CHILD IS BEING BULLIED?

1. The first thing you can do is help your child talk about what is happening. Being specific about your worries can help a reluctant child open up: 'I notice you have been very unhappy going to school the last few days. Is there anything or anyone bothering you in school?'

2. Listen to your child's feelings about what has happened and be there to support them emotionally – remember, this is as important as taking action to stop the bullying. Crucially, reassure your child that he/she is not at fault for the bullying – he/she does not deserve to be bullied.

3. Be careful about overreacting to what your child discloses, either by becoming very upset yourself or by immediately rushing in a rage to the school to demand action. Impulsive actions can make matters worse and can make your child reluctant to talk to you.

4. Make a plan of action to deal with the bullying (such as meeting with the school or contacting the website host in the case of online bullying). Seek professional support and guidance as necessary.

5. Depending on your child's age, think through with them what actions they can take to protect themselves or to stop the bullying (e.g. keeping away from the bullies, being assertive in response to the bully's taunts, or talking to the teachers). However, be wary about thinking that children can solve the bullying themselves – because of the power dynamics most children will need the support of an adult to stop the bullying.

6. Remember to support your child's friendship with other children who are kind to them. Also, encourage your child's involvement in other healthy and enjoyable pursuits that provide respite and another source of support to them.

WHAT TO DO IF YOU SUSPECT YOUR CHILD IS A BULLY

1. Take seriously any report that your child might be bullying others. Don't underreact by dismissing the suggestion ('my child would never do such a thing') or overreact by being very punitive towards

your child. The key is to intervene early to stop the pattern and help your child learn better ways of communicating or fitting in with a group.

2. Present the information directly to your child and listen carefully to their account of what is happening as well as their own feelings.

3. Focus on the alleged bullying behaviour that you want to stop and not your child 'being a bully'. Help them think of the impact of the behaviour on the other child and to imagine how they might feel in the same situation. Emphasise the importance of respect, accepting and including others.

4. Explore actions your child can take to move forward (such as apologising if appropriate) or communication skills they can use to stop the bullying. For example, if it occurs in a group, explore what they might say or do to stop it, e.g. address the person who starts it, 'Come on, don't be stupid. Leave John alone.'

5. Hold them accountable for their behaviour and warn them of further consequences (e.g. loss of privileges) if they don't stop.

6. Monitor the situation carefully and make sure to check in again with your child as to how things are going. In addition, work cooperatively with the school or whoever made the report to sort things out.

A SCHOOL-BASED COMMUNITY RESPONSE

The key to dealing with bullying is to break the silence and to address it early before it becomes a pattern for both the bully or victim, and also the wider group that might support it. Schools have a particular responsibility in addressing bullying, by having proactive positive behaviour and anti-bullying policies in place. Such policies should have a preventative component, such as educating children about the dangers of bullying as well as teaching appropriate communication skills, both face-to-face and within the online world of social media. In addition, because of the silence surrounding bullying, schools need to actively encourage children to report incidents whether they are bystanders or victims to it. In this regard, some schools adopt creative approaches such as conducting frequent anonymous surveys with pupils about incidents of bullying and most importantly following these up. In addition, schools need to act immediately to address reports of bullying. Such actions include skilled interviewing of the alleged bully (see above), and the use of school sanctions in a proportionate way as well as skilled interventions in the classroom in cases of group bullying.

My sixteen-year-old daughter is being bullied online

Q. *My sixteen-year-old daughter has become quite withdrawn and irritable the last few weeks. She eventually told me that she was picked on and bullied by another girl online. This girl is from the area we live in, though she goes to another school. My daughter met a boy at a disco a few months go and dated him a few times. He was an ex-boyfriend of this girl and she posted some nasty stuff about my daughter online. My daughter got angry and retaliated online and then it escalated and the other girl shared the comments with other people. My daughter was very upset but seems to be better now we have talked. I'm not sure if I should do anything now (a friend says I should report it) as it seems to have quietened down and there are no further posts online. Also my daughter was a little culpable as she said some nasty stuff back to the other girl.*

A. While young people have always been falling out and saying mean things about one another, your question highlights how this problem can be made a lot worse when these disputes occur online. Comments posted on social networking websites have much greater potential to hurt as they can be more widely distributed and form a permanent record on the internet. Furthermore, there is evidence that people can be more uninhibited online and likely to make more virulent and nasty comments than they would in face-to-face communication.

It is good that your daughter spoke to you about what happened to her and that you were there to support her. Having an understanding ally in a parent makes such a difference to young people dealing with difficult social situations like this one. What to do next really depends on how serious an incident it was, how your daughter is affected and whether it will be repeated. If there has been no recent follow-up then the best thing may be to let things lie for the moment and help your daughter learn from what happened and move on. There is a lot for her to learn about understanding jealousy in romantic relationships and also how to deal with difficult people online. As it may be a one-off incident, and in the context of a relationship dispute, there may be no need to report it but you should skill keep a record of the communications in case you need to take action in the future. Below I list some tips for parents on how to prevent and deal with online bullying that you might want to discuss with your daughter:

EMPHASISE THE IMPORTANCE OF RESPECTFUL COMMUNICATION ONLINE

Rather than waiting for problems, it is important to discuss with young people the etiquette for communicating online. It is important for them to be aware of how banter or mildly negative comments can be perceived as offensive when written online. In fact, in order to avoid offence everyone needs to be much more careful about what they post online than what they might say in face-to-face communication. In addition, you need to remind young people that comments made impulsively can get them into trouble, and this will be more so in the future as guidelines around online bullying in schools become more enforced.

TELL A TRUSTED ADULT

Encourage your children to tell you or a trusted adult if they witness nasty comments or bullying behaviour online. Dealing with issues alone or keeping things secret fuels bullying. Telling a supportive adult is a really important step in breaking isolation and in gaining support to take appropriate action.

BE IN CONTROL OF HOW YOU RESPOND

It is important that young people don't retaliate or overreact to bullying online. It is tempting to 'give as good as you get' if you feel mistreated, or alternatively to plead with the person who is making the comments to stop. However, such responses may fuel the bullying behaviour and could also get the young person into trouble. Sometimes it is best to show no response, to block the person from communicating, and to tell someone trustworthy what is happening. At other times, it may be helpful to communicate assertively and to warn the person making the comments by saying something like, 'What you have posted is untrue, please take those comments down or I will report you.' Encourage your teenagers to talk with you, so you can plan a response together.

DON'T COLLUDE WITH BULLYING

It is also important to teach young people not to collude with or be a bystander to bullying online. They can be encouraged not to read or share bullying comments about others, as well as enabled to challenge others bullying online, perhaps by defending a person or telling people to stop posting nasty comments about others. Young people regulating their own communication is the best way to eliminate bullying in the long term. There are some good resources for young people working together to eliminate bullying, such as watchyourspace.ie. You could review those resources together with your daughter.

REPORT BULLYING IF IT PERSISTS

If the bullying persists you should of course consider reporting the person to the relevant social networking website, to school authorities if it is in a school context, or to the internet service provider, and also to the police in serious cases. For this reason, you should always keep records of communication in case the situation escalates.

HELP YOUR TEENAGER PUT THINGS IN PERSPECTIVE

As a parent you can't protect your child from all negative experiences but you can help them think through the issues and respond appropriately. Just because someone calls them names does not make these things true, and it says more about the other person's problems than their own. By helping your teenagers put things in perspective, you can help preserve their self-esteem and to aid them in learning from the experience.

My thirteen-year-old son has Asperger's and can't make friends

Q. *I have a thirteen-year-old boy with Asperger's syndrome. It has always been a challenge to bring him up, but it has become much harder since he has become a teenager. He has no friends, finds school very hard socially (though seems to be doing okay academically) and, although he doesn't say as much, I think he feels very alone. I worry a lot about him and the future. How can I help him?*

A. Asperger's syndrome (AS) is an autism spectrum disorder which results in children having particular difficulties in social relationships (often finding it hard to empathise and read people) as well as social communication (often missing subtle communications such as humour, tone of voice, etc). In addition, children and young people with AS tend to have restricted or repetitive interests, can find change harder than most (preferring rigid routines) and some have particular sensory sensitivities (for example, finding noisy rooms more distressing than other people). Children with AS are at least average or above-average intelligence and many can cope with and do well in mainstream school.

Adolescence can be a particularly difficult time for a child with AS, when fitting into peer groups and making friends becomes centrally important. Getting on with peers the same age can be very hard for teens with AS and this can cause them to 'cut off' or to become more isolated than before. Being acutely aware of this, they can often become depressed at this time and may need more support than the average teenager in managing all of these issues.

HELPING YOUR SON MAKE FRIENDS

As his parents, there are a lot of different things you can do to help. The long-term aim is to help your son find his niche in life and friends who accept him for who he is. Helping him mix with other people who share his special interests and hobbies can be a good start. Lots of young people with AS find mixing with teenagers the same age the hardest, where fitting in and knowing the social code is at its most pronounced. However, it can be easier to get on with younger or older teens or even adults who may be less judgemental, particularly if they share the same interests and hobbies. If your son is interested in chess, for example, he is more likely to find his niche and a more accepting social group within a chess club that includes lots of different age groups.

You can also support him in making friends by persisting in exposing him to new social opportunities that ideally match his interests and facilitating him making contact with or visiting any potential friends. If he is open to the idea, you can also coach him in the social skills needed to make friends. For example, you can discuss with him the skills of approaching new kids, such as waiting for a good time to talk and making sure to first ask about what they are interested in before launching into his own special topic. Or you can help him learn to judge other people's emotions in social situations, as well as learning strategies to appropriately express his own feelings.

USING RESOURCES AND GETTING SUPPORT

There are lots of very good social skills workbooks and books for teens and young adults with AS that look at these very topics. These include *The Social Success Workbook for Teens* by Barbara Cooper, which looks at skill-building activities for teens with AS and other social skill problems, and *Succeeding in College with Asperger Syndrome – A Student Guide* by John Harpur, which is suitable for older teens.

In addition, there are some good Irish support organisations such as Aspire (aspireireland.ie) or Autism Support Ireland (autismsupport. ie) that contain useful information and details of available services. For example, Aspire runs drama classes for children and young people with AS which may be suitable for your son.

Another important source of support is your son's school, which you should consider contacting to discuss your concerns. The fact that he is doing well in school is an advantage, and they might be able to support him making friends and even identify possible peer groups within the classroom or after-school groups where he might be more likely to fit in and enjoy himself.

TALK TO YOUR SON ABOUT ASPERGER'S SYNDROME

If you have not done so already, it might be useful to sit down with him and discuss what AS means and to listen to how he feels about the diagnosis and how he wants to approach the problems he encounters. This is a delicate conversation, but if handled it well it can help him understand how he is different and the challenges this brings, but also the benefits or particular strengths he has. You could also point him in the direction of some of the positive role models of people with AS who have made a great contribution in society. Many creative geniuses – such as Albert Einstein and W. B. Yeats – are considered by some experts to have been on the autistic spectrum. Once again, there are many great books which describe the experience of having AS that you could read with your son, including personal accounts written by teenagers such as *Freaks, Geeks and Asperger Syndrome* by Luke Jackson or comprehensive professional accounts by leading experts such as *The Complete Guide to Asperger's Syndrome* by Tony Attwood. In addition, there are many forums and blogs on the internet that promote a positive view of AS for teenagers and allow them to gain mutual support.

Parenting a child with AS is challenging at the best of times and the teenage years bring new worries and concerns, such as making friendships, forging a career or living independently in the future. While it is easy to feel alone, it is important to realise that many parents have gone through what you are experiencing. I recommend you make contact with the support organisations listed previously. In general, parents rate the advice, support and information from other parents bringing up children with AS as the most valuable.

My fourteen-year-old daughter can't make friends

Q. *We have three children, a girl aged fourteen, a boy aged eleven and a girl aged four. The eldest seems to have great difficulty in making friends. She is in second year in a mixed sex school and just cannot seem to fit in with any group. We have suggested many things, such as joining sports groups, which she has done, but on a daily basis she says she is excluded and comes home very unhappy. She is in a hockey club outside school and seems happier* *there. She's in a drama group, also outside school, and is more confident meeting new people in these settings. She seems stuck in a rut in school and she feels she is carrying a reputation for being unpopular. She struggled to have friends in primary school, so this seems to be an extension of her difficulties. We find it so upsetting when she asks if she will ever have friends. She says she hates her life. We try to advise her but mostly she gets very upset or can get very angry and shout at us. I am not sure what to suggest for her – we'd appreciate some advice.*

A. As a parent, it is hard to witness your child having difficulties with friendships – you can see their unhappiness, yet it is not something you can directly control. Though you can support them, you can't make friends for them and this is something they have to do for themselves. Friendships can be particularly challenging during adolescence, when teenagers are working out their own identity and how to fit in with their peer group, and this can be particularly hard in school. While as an adult you have control over your social and work groups, as a teenager you can't choose your classmates. You share the school with them whether you get on with them or not.

REACH OUT AND OFFER SUPPORT
As a parent, there is a lot you can do to help your daughter. The place to start is making sure you are there to listen and support her. Though it can be distressing to see her upset, it is good that your daughter shares her feelings with you and it would be far worse if she bottled things up and spoke to no one. Even though she might initially react angrily to your offers of help, it is important that you continually reach out to her and support her. During the teenage years, children are pulling away from their parents and can be less likely to accept direct advice or influence, so you often need to adapt your approach.

HELP HER COME UP WITH SOLUTIONS
When your daughter talks about things, be wary about giving too much advice or jumping in to sort out the problem. Instead, any time she talks, make an effort to first listen patiently and empathise with her, before

helping her come up with solutions. It can help to explore with her exactly what is happening in the classroom, to identify the different groups and subgroups and when/how she feels excluded, etc. It is also useful to explore whether there are boys or girls in the class who she gets on better with, or if there are any classes or times she feels more comfortable and included. You may be able to identify some girls or boys in the class with whom she might have more in common and those who could be potential friends.

EXPLORE CONCRETE STRATEGIES FOR MAKING FRIENDS

If your daughter is open to this, you could explore concrete strategies for making new friends and coping in school, whether this is how to break the ice and approach a new person, or how to join in a game or conversation, or how to listen and share interests and so on. There are some good books on friendships and coping as a teenager that you could read with your daughter, such as *The Seven Habits of Highly Effective Teens* by Sean Covey. In addition, forming friendships is a topic that is regularly covered in teenage magazines and sitcoms – maybe you could read, watch and discuss these with your daughter as a starting point to talking through the issues.

LINK IN WITH YOUR DAUGHTER'S SCHOOL

It is also a good idea to talk to the teachers in your daughter's school about how she is getting on and what they can do to support her (this is ideally done with your daughter's knowledge). Schools have a responsibility to ensure no bullying or exclusion occurs and there are lot of things that teachers can sensitively do such as keeping a close eye on class interactions, making subtle changes in the classroom to support your daughter fitting in more, as well as helping her get involved in activities or giving her a position of responsibility. Some schools may also have a school counsellor that your daughter could see confidentially for more regular support in managing the situation.

BUILD HER SELF-ESTEEM IN OTHER AREAS OF HER LIFE

It is also important to build on what is working outside the school. The fact that she is happier and making friends in hockey and drama is great and something to cultivate. Maybe you could allow her more time in these activities and support these friendships? You could also help her to meet other friends outside school, for example, by arranging family events where your daughter spends time with cousins or friends' children of her own age whom she might like. Continue to build her self-esteem in other areas of her life and set up situations where she can find her niche. For example, taking up a creative hobby or volunteering for a good cause, or taking a challenge such as working to achieve a Gaisce award are all activities which will not only make her feel better about herself but bring her into contact with new friends.

KEEP YOUR OWN RELATIONSHIP WITH HER POSITIVE

Many children go through periods of unhappiness or poor friendships in school, and what gets them through is the fact that they have a good life outside school, either in other interests or in a close connection with their family. Whatever happens, make sure to cultivate your own relationship with your daughter. Set aside time to be with her one to one, doing fun stuff and not just talking about problems. Whatever difficulties your daughter has with friends, being close to her parents will be crucial respite for her and help her succeed in the long term.

SMOKING, DRINKING AND DRUGS

I think my thirteen-year-old daughter is smoking

Q. *I think my thirteen-year-old daughter, who has just begun second year, has started smoking. One day last week, when she came in from school, I got the whiff of smoke from her. When I asked her was she smoking, she denied it and gave an elaborate story, which I didn't believe, but left it at that. Two nights later, I searched her room and did find a packet hidden with a few cigarettes in it. I asked her about them and she said she was minding them for a friend (a fifteen year old), which I didn't believe either. I really hope she isn't smoking (I'm an ex-smoker myself) and am wondering how to approach this when she keeps denying it. She is a good girl otherwise, does well at school, has good friends, although she is a bit impressionable and easily led by them.*

A. From what you describe, it does sound like your daughter is smoking or is at least experimenting with it. You are right to be concerned as a parent, as the younger a child starts smoking, the more likely they are to become hooked and the higher the risk of problems.

THE IMPORTANCE OF INTERVENING EARLY TO STOP SMOKING BECOMING A HABIT

It is also important to try to intervene early, as your daughter may have tried only one or two cigarettes and may not yet have developed a habit. (While it is unlikely, she may not have even smoked a cigarette yet, though she is clearly at risk of doing so.) The earlier she pulls back from smoking the easier it will be for her to stop, as although she may still have to deal with a smoking peer group, she won't have the difficulty of overcoming an addiction.

RAISING THE SUBJECT WITH HER

You are right to think carefully about how best to respond, especially when your daughter is consistently denying any problem. You can help her open up and talk about things by directly (though gently) confronting her: 'Whatever you are saying, it does seem to me that you might be smoking and this is something I am worried about.' If she gives excuses or continues to deny it, you can persist: 'Even if you are minding them for a friend, it is not acceptable at all that you are keeping cigarettes in the house. Either way we need to talk about it.' Of course, the ideal is that she would talk to you honestly about whether she has smoked and the circumstances of this, though you can still address the issue and take steps to ensure she is safe even if she continues her denial.

STRATEGIES TO HELP HER QUIT

In helping her quit, a number of different approaches can be taken, such as being empathic and supportive as well as being clear about rules and expectations. For example, you can be understanding about the pressures to smoke and her desire to fit in, but you can be clear that at thirteen she is too young to do so and your preference is that she does not smoke at all, due to the potential health problems. When expressing your concerns, it is important to match your explanation to what might motivate her. For example, at thirteen she might not be as troubled by the serious long-term health problems, though she might be upset at some of the unattractive aspects of smoking, such as stained fingernails, bad breath, or lack of fitness if she is motivated to play sports.

If she is a free-thinking person, she might be put out by how she is being manipulated to buy cigarettes by the subtle advertising of the companies that sell them. She also might be inspired by your own story of how you regretted smoking and how you finally gave them up. When having this conversation, it is important to ask her questions, to listen and to check what she thinks. You could also go online together to check the various websites discussing the problems surrounding smoking and how to avoid it.

HELP HER DEAL WITH PEER PRESSURE

It is also important to check if she is being pressured into smoking by a peer group. In this case, it is important to explore how she can resist this.

Lots of teens start smoking or engaging in other dangerous behaviours because they don't know how to say no to their peer group. Help her think how she can say no in a way that gains her respect, and also how she might be better off with other friends who respect her making her own decisions.

USING DISCIPLINE STRATEGIES TO HELP HER QUIT
Given she is only thirteen, you should consider your discipline options to prevent her smoking. For example, you could be more vigilant about who she is going out with and where she is going. You can be clear with her that until you are convinced she is not smoking, you will be restricting her freedom and that she has to earn her privileges at home by taking steps to stop smoking.

Also, as smoking is expensive, you need to check where she is getting money and take action to stop the supply. You can be clear with her that she will only get pocket money when you know for sure she is not smoking. You can also set a positive goal and then reward her if she makes an effort. For example, you could tell her that if she avoids smoking for the next two or three months, you will buy her something special or support her making a trip and so on.

GAINING EXTRA SUPPORT
If smoking has become a habit for her and she needs support to overcome it, you could explore with her the various options and programmes that could help her quit. A good place to start is the National Smokers' Quitline at 1850 201 203 or quit.ie. The helpline may also provide more information as to how you, as a parent, can influence your daughter to stop smoking.

Should I allow my sixteen-year-old son to start drinking alcohol?
Q. *My son has just turned sixteen and has been telling me that his friends have started drinking and he's been joking that he should be allowed to drink too. He's also been asking to go to house parties where I'm sure there will be drinking going on. Some of my friends have advised me that I should let him have a drink at home rather than having him do it behind my back. I'm not sure about doing this, and would greatly value your opinion.*

A. You are right to be concerned about this issue. Teen binge drinking and all the associated problems have been on the increase in recent years in Ireland. Many surveys have found that teenagers are drinking earlier and more heavily than their counterparts a decade or two ago.

PARENTS ARE KEY IN REDUCING PROBLEMATIC DRINKING

While, of course, media influences and peer pressure are variables in teenage drinking, parents have a crucial role in influencing teenagers positively to delay drinking until they are older and in reducing problematic drinking when they start. Good supervision, role-modelling and effective parent–child communication are all key factors in helping your teen avoid problems with alcohol.

In tackling teenage drinking, parents are often faced with dilemmas such as the ones you describe. Should I allow my teen to go to parties where there is drinking? Should I allow my teen to drink at home where I can supervise him? In considering these questions, it is worth looking at some of the research in relation to problematic drinking. The biggest predictor of later problems with alcohol for young adults is the age they start drinking. The earlier your teen starts to drink, the more likely they are to go on to have problems (and to go on to use other drugs).

HELP YOUR TEEN DELAY STARTING TO DRINK

As a parent, a very important goal is to try to get your teen to delay starting to drink until as late as possible. Though some teenagers may start to drink earlier, personally I think the legal age of eighteen years is the standard to aim for. It is important to sit down with your teenagers and to state your values in this regard. A lot of parents are afraid to raise the subject, but telling your teen that you'd prefer that they did not drink until they are older, and explaining your positive reasons for this, sends out a very clear signal.

For this reason, I am not sure that supervised drinking at home is a good idea for teenagers as it sends out a mixed message. Of course, teenagers may go behind your back and choose to experiment with drinking, but they are less likely to do this if they know your clear preference in this regard.

PARENTAL SUPERVISION IS VERY IMPORTANT

Good supervision is also very important. When young teenagers are going to parties you need to check where they will be going, agree when they will be back, make sure they have their phone on, and so on. It is okay to have a rule that they should not be going to parties where drink is freely available unless they can convince you that they can be trusted and will not join in.

TALK TO YOUR TEENAGERS ABOUT THE PROBLEMS ASSOCIATED WITH DRINKING

It is also useful to have conversations with your teenager about the dangers of alcohol and drugs and to be proactive in this regard. Some studies have shown that children whose parents openly discuss issues such as drugs/ alcohol are less likely to experiment with drugs or have problematic drinking when they are older – it is important that they are getting information from you and not just from the media and their peer group.

These conversations don't have to be formal affairs. When your teen jokes about being allowed to drink, this can be a time to start a conversation, or you might open a discussion when the topic comes up on the news or even during a soap opera or in a movie. The best approach is to listen to a teenager's opinion first, before sharing your own values. For example, if a storyline in a soap opera focuses on teen drinking, you can ask your son different questions such as, 'What do you think of what is happening?' or 'How safe is that teenager?' or 'What would you do in the same situation?'

HELP YOUR SON DEAL WITH PEER PRESSURE AROUND DRINKING

An equally important conversation to have with your son is around dealing with peer pressure. In research on school programmes to prevent early smoking, drinking or drug taking, the most successful approaches were not ones that simply focused on highlighting the dangers of these behaviours but also ones that taught young people how to assert themselves, to resist peer pressure and to say no to their peers in a positive way. For example, it is useful to discuss with your son what would he do if someone offered him drugs? Or what would he say if he felt pressured to do something that he didn't want to? In the future, you can use these conversations to explore safe drinking with him, for example, asking him how could he ensure he was safe if he went to a party or how would he know a safe level of drinking or which friends could he trust most when he was out? Talking through the issues with your son and helping him think up options and strategies is a good way to help him be safe in the long term.

So, to summarise, the best approach to helping your teenager with alcohol is to delay their starting to drink as late as possible, and when they start, to help them to do this in a safe and social way. Being realistic, the message to give your teenagers is, 'Be good, and if you can't be good, be careful.'

In addition, it is important to always supervise your teenagers in line with their age and check in on them to ensure there is regular contact between you. Above all, make sure the lines of communication are always open, and give them the message that no matter what happens they can turn to you for support and guidance.

I am worried my seventeen-year-old is using drugs

Q. *I think my seventeen-year-old has started using cannabis and I am worried. Last week when I was cleaning his room, I found some of the paraphernalia for smoking cannabis. When I confronted him he went ballistic that I was 'searching' his room and then denied he was smoking, before storming off. Since then he hasn't been talking to me. I don't know what to believe. We have caught him using cannabis once in the past, about a year ago, and he assured us it was a one-off. More recently, I have been worried about him, as he has been more secretive and hanging out with a group of friends I disapprove of. He also has been demotivated in school (he's now in his Leaving Cert year), so he is showing all the worrying signs.*

A. Cannabis is the most common illegally used drug in Ireland, with just over a quarter of young adults reporting to have used it at some point in their lives. As a parent you are right to be concerned as long-term use of cannabis is associated with demotivation and mental health problems. However, it is important to weigh up the situation with your son and to consider how serious his drug use might be so you can decide how best to help him. There is a big difference between a young person experimenting with cannabis and someone who has developed a significant habit or who may have become addicted.

RAISING THE SUBJECT WITH YOUR SON ABOUT HIS DRUG USE

Though you are not talking to your son at the moment it is important to try and raise the issue again with him. Pick your moment and try to approach the subject in a concerned non-confrontational way: 'Listen, we need to talk about what I found in your room. As your parent, it is my job to be concerned for you.' If he remains defensive, ask him what would he do if he were the parent and discovered evidence of drugs in his son's room. The ideal is to get him to open up and talk about his drug use, but you might have to give him a bit of time to do this. Make sure not to overreact or judge him whatever details he begins to tell you. Even if he doesn't admit things or continues to argue that he is not using drugs, you can still talk in third-party terms about the dangers of drug use and how to keep safe.

DISCUSS THE DANGERS OF DRUG USE

In discussing the dangers of drugs, the ideal is to get your son to self-challenge and to think through the issues for himself. Ask him what he thinks the implications for his health are and about the problems with it being illegal. Express your concerns for him positively – for example, how you worry that using drugs will negatively impact his health and schoolwork and stop him achieving his goals in life.

AGREE A PLAN FOR KEEPING SAFE

Try to come up with a plan for keeping him safe from drugs. This can include avoiding certain peer groups or social situations where he might be under pressure to use drugs, or encouraging him to concentrate on more healthy pursuits. It could also involve helping him to be more assertive and to say no in certain situations, as well as seeking counselling individually or as a family. The ideal, of course, is for him to agree to this plan and for you to help him carry it out, but even if he does not there are still things you can do to help keep him safe. For example, you can increase your vigilance and monitoring of his whereabouts, or make pocket money or other privileges dependent on him engaging more positively in school or other activities. If he resists your rules you can say these measures are only temporary until you rebuild some trust with him and are more sure he is not using drugs.

KEEP POSITIVE AND ENCOURAGE HIM IN OTHER ASPECTS OF HIS LIFE

Independent of whatever drug use he might be involved in, continue to positively encourage him to engage in other healthy and positive aspects of his life, such as engaging in school or sport or healthy hobbies or voluntary work or anything else that might be a positive influence in his life.

KEEP THE LINES OF COMMUNICATION OPEN BETWEEN YOU

Whatever happens, work hard at keeping the lines of communication open. Don't let this drive a wedge between you or become the only issue in your relationship with him. Continue to reach out and connect with him. Take an interest in what he enjoys and try to have a daily time of checking in with him that is not just focused on monitoring or disciplining him but rather on building a relationship. In the long term, it is the quality of your relationship that will give you the best chance of positively influencing him.

SEEK OUTSIDE HELP AND SUPPORT

Finally there are a range of counselling and advice services that may be helpful to you and your son, such as the drugs helpline on 1800 459 459 or www.drugs.ie. Even if your son does not initially engage, you can make contact as a concerned parent for advice and support.

SEXUALITY AND DATING

I found sex texts on my daughter's phone

Q. *The other night when my daughter, who is sixteen, went out, she left her phone behind. I know I shouldn't have, but curiosity got the better of me and I looked through her texts. I just wanted to check she was okay because she hasn't been communicating a lot with me lately. However, I was shocked at what I discovered. On the phone were a number of sexually explicit texts between her and a boy in the local area. It was clear that they had met up a few times as boyfriend and girlfriend and although they hadn't gone 'all the way', they had come pretty close. I don't know what upsets me most about all of this. I am shocked at the sexual talk and worried that she might be about to have sex when she is far too young and not prepared in any way. Should I try to stop her relationship with this boy or am I overreacting about what I have discovered? Is this what all teenagers are up to?*

A. When concerned about their teenager's welfare or simply feeling disconnected from them, many parents resort to checking their texts, emails and internet history. While the ideal is that your teenager would tell you what is going on in their life or come to you if they were experiencing a difficult situation, this is not always the case. Of course, age is a significant issue here. For a child or young teenager, it is perfectly appropriate for a parent to check what they are doing online and on their phones; in fact, this can be an upfront rule that might be even a condition of use – for example, your child is only allowed to use email if she is open about what she is sending and so on.

However, as a teenager becomes older they are entitled to privacy and it is normal and appropriate that they might not discuss all details of their life with their parents, especially their dating and sexual experiences. But you still have a responsibility to do what you can to ensure they are safe.

HOW TO RAISE THE SUBJECT WITH YOUR DAUGHTER

Deciding what to do next is a delicate matter. Some people might advise that you should not tell her that you read her texts for fear that this might breach her trust, and instead suggest you simply raise some of the issues you are concerned about with her, picking a time to talk to her about relationships, boyfriends, sex, safety and so on.

My own view is that it might be best to come clean and to tell her you read her texts and this is the reason for the chat. You could say something like, 'When you were out I read some of the texts on your phone. There was something that worried me in a few of them that we need to have a chat about.'

Think through what you might say if she objects to you reading her texts, for example, 'I only read them because I was worried about you and needed to check you were okay.' If she is too upset initially to talk, you can come back to the conversation later.

DISCUSSING SEX WITH YOUR DAUGHTER

When you do talk it is important to first listen to her perspective. Use questions to help her open up. How long has she been seeing this boy? How are things going in the relationship? Then talk to her about your concerns and the issues for you, such as how it was not okay for her to keep the relationship secret, the importance of being ready for sex, about the law and the age of consent being seventeen, and about safe sex and birth control. If she objects to this conversation, you could say that, as her parent, you have to ensure she is safe and that you wouldn't be doing your job well otherwise.

It is important to feel free to express your values to your daughter. Don't be put off by the idea that 'this is what all teenagers are up to' – you are entitled as a parent to say how you think it best for her to behave. In fact, most teenagers, though they might disagree, respect parents being clear with them about rules and even see it as a sign of care for them.

If you feel she should wait until she is older before she has a boyfriend or if you feel she is too young to be having sex, then say that this is what you think is best for her. In terms of what action you should take, a lot depends on how your conversation goes and how much trust is established.

EMPOWERING YOUR DAUGHTER TO MAKE HER OWN DECISIONS

The ideal is for her to take action herself; for example, encouraging her to reflect on whether she is comfortable in the relationship or whether she should maybe even decide to cool things down. As a parent you could, of course, set some rules about safety and going out – for example, that she is supervised and collected – and also take extra steps to check where she is going and so on. However, be realistic about what you can do with rules alone; the goal is to try to gain her cooperation.

There are some useful Irish resources and websites on the subject of helping teens make responsible decisions about sex, such as www.b4udecide.ie. You could access these as a parent, recommend them to your daughter or even read them together.

Finally, though finding your daughter's texts may be a distressing event, it is also an opportunity to raise some important issues with her and it could be the start of some important conversations between you.

At what age should my daughter go to a disco?

Q. *There is a teenage disco in our local area and my thirteen-year-old daughter is very keen to go. Though it seems to be well organised and targeted at first years, I feel a bit reluctant about letting her go. I might be a bit old-fashioned but I think thirteen is too young. I also worry about what goes on at these discos with the way the girls dress in an over-sexualised way and all that might go on with the boys. My daughter is a sensible girl who hasn't given me much trouble. She would accept it if I said no but she says she would feel really left out. She says nearly her whole class are going as well as her close friends and this seems to be the case when I check. I'm not sure what to do. As I am parenting alone and she is my eldest I haven't had to deal with these issues before.*

A. Pushing for independence is the mark of the teenage years and the best response as a parent is neither saying an immediate 'yes' nor an immediate 'no' to each of your teenager's requests. Instead, the key is to negotiate independence gradually with your teenager and to use each request for more responsibility as an opportunity to reflect about and think through issues and to prepare your teenager to take a next step in living their own lives. As a result, it is important to take your daughter's request to go to the disco seriously and to consider all the issues with her before deciding.

THINK THROUGH ISSUES AND CHECK IN WITH OTHER PARENTS

Dealing with your eldest entering the teenage years is unknown territory as a parent, and it is particularly hard if you are parenting alone or without support. You might find it useful to talk things through with a close friend or with other parents you trust. For example, it would be reasonable to make contact with one or more of your daughter's friends' parents to discuss the pros and cons of the disco and to share concerns. This way you can put things in perspective and reduce your own anxiety. Certainly, making contact with other parents could help ensure your daughter's safety as it allows you to check who she might be going with and to share the supervision of the teenagers when travelling to and from the disco.

LISTEN TO YOUR DAUGHTER'S PERSPECTIVE

Don't prejudge your daughter's motives for going to the disco or start by giving her lots of warnings about the dangers. Take time to listen and to understand what it means for her. For some girls, socialising with boys is a big feature of going to a first disco but others may simply be interested in the ritual of dressing up, showing off their new clothes, dancing and having fun with their friends. The more you understand what it means to her, the more you will be able to decide if she is ready to go, what preparation she might need and also to present alternative options if you need to. It is a valid reason that she may want to go because 'all her friends' are going, as fitting in and being part of the group is an important issue for teenagers, though you should also check that she is not only going to please friends and help her make other plans if that is what she wants.

BE PREPARED TO SET RULES AND CONDITIONS

Whatever you decide, it is important that you are prepared to set rules that focus on your daughter's safety; for example, making sure that she is going with good friends and that she is supervised when travelling to and from the venue. If you have not done so already, do start a conversation about sex and relationships with her, emphasising not only information but also the values you want her to have. With a young teenager it is reasonable for you to set some rules about how she dresses and what make-up she wears, and to make these conditions of her going to the disco.

DISCUSS SAFETY WITH YOUR DAUGHTER

A good approach with teenagers is to not simply lecture them about the dangers they might be exposed to but instead explore how they might deal with difficult situations. For example, as well as expressing your own views, ask your daughter what she thinks of how the girls dress and how the boys respond, or what she thinks the problems are for boys and girls dating at a young age. You could also explore what she might do in a difficult situation, such as how she might react if a boy gave her unwanted attention or how she would say no if someone put pressure on her to drink alcohol. Over time, you want to help her make her own decisions, to set her own limits and not to feel pressured in any way.

TRY TO TRUST YOUR DAUGHTER

Going out to a first disco or social event can be an important rite of passage for a young teenager and something that marks them growing up. If you feel that your daughter is a sensible girl then it can be helpful to trust her and to give her some freedom on this occasion, especially as you feel the disco is well supervised and a safe place for her to socialise. Make sure to check in with her when the event is over, as keeping connected with her is very important as she grows up. Above all, make sure to keep the channels of communication open between you so she knows that she can always come and talk to you if she is worried about anything.

I think my son might be gay

Q. *I think my fourteen-year-old son, who is an only child, might be gay. It is something I always had in the back of my mind, but now I feel there are more definite signs in what he is saying and what he is wearing etc. To be honest, I feel I would be fine about it. I would worry a lot for him though. We live in* *a small rural town and I'd worry that he would get picked on or bullied if he came out as being gay. I think my husband, who is very religious, will have a bigger problem if our son is gay. When I raised the possibility directly with my husband, he was clearly uncomfortable and dismissed angrily what I was saying. I want to do what's best for my son. Should I ask him directly or wait until he tells me himself?*

A. While it is impossible for you to know what your son's sexual orientation is (this is something private for him to work out), it is good that you are trying to be sensitive about this important issue.

THE CHALLENGES FOR TEENAGERS WHO MAY BE GAY

Whether straight or gay, lots of teenagers struggle with their sexuality as they work out who they are. Teenagers who finally identify themselves as gay, lesbian or bisexual, often find the teenage years particularly challenging as they can feel left out and isolated, especially if they live in families or communities where there are no positive gay or lesbian role models and where there might be widespread homophobia. Indeed, the stress on these teenagers can be great, and they are at a higher risk of depression and other problems. In helping your son through these issues, the important thing is to give him the message that you love and accept him no matter what his sexuality is.

RAISING THE SUBJECT WITH HIM

However, it is a delicate issue as to how direct you should be in raising the subject of sexuality with him. If you asked him directly whether he was gay or not, though he might be relieved that the subject is in the open, he also might be deeply embarrassed. He could even react negatively or feel insulted by the question. At fourteen, he might still be working out his sexual feelings and coming to terms with his orientation, and not be ready for a direct conversation with his mother about it.

In the first instance, it might be better if you are more indirect and subtle in your communication. For example, if the subject came up on the TV or in a newspaper article, you could express a supportive and sensitive view about being gay and communicate the view that people should be accepted and not judged for their sexual orientation.

You could also speak positively about gay role models in the media, in your local community or even within the extended family and listen to anything he says about the subject. Many teens will sound out their parents to see if they will respond supportively before they tell them something difficult or important in their lives. The key is to give your son the message, indirectly or directly, that you won't have a problem if he is gay and that you love him regardless. Many gay teenagers draw comfort from the fact that their parents are okay about their sexuality and it does make it easier for them to come out when they are ready.

DEALING WITH HOMOPHOBIA

In your question, you also ask about how your son might be treated if he came out as gay. This is a concern as male teenage culture can still be quite homophobic and a teenager who comes out could be at risk of being bullied. This is especially the case in peer groups that can't be chosen, such as in the classroom. Though there has been a lot of progress in recent times, and schools and youth groups try to promote a more positive culture, it makes sense that young people should be cautious about who and when they tell, and make sure to start with friends and family members they trust.

COMING TO TERMS AS PARENTS

Even though you might feel that you would be okay with the possibility that your son is gay, it is important to acknowledge that for many parents this would be a great adjustment. Just like most teens who are gay themselves take some time to come to terms with this fact, so too do their parents.

For many parents, it is often initially experienced as a loss, in that they have to envision a different future for their children that they were not expecting. There are some good Irish organisations, such as www.belongto.org, that provide information and support, both for parents and teens adjusting to being lesbian, gay, bisexual or transgender that you may be interested in contacting now or later.

If your son did come out as gay, his father might find this more difficult than most, especially if he has traditional views about sexuality. If in the future your son does indicate that he is gay and wants to tell his father, it might be a good idea for you to first talk this through with your husband and help him prepare how to respond. Even if parents have initial difficulty with accepting their child's orientation, their love for their child is greater and they can still communicate a positive message. If your husband is religious, there are many religious groups that promote a compassionate understanding of homosexuality that he may be interested in finding out more about, such as the Lesbian and Gay Christian movement (www.lgcm.org.uk).

Finally, it is important to acknowledge that you may be jumping the gun with your worries about your son's sexuality. While it is important that you prepare yourself to be sensitive and understanding as to what your son might tell you, it is also important to give him time and space (as well as privacy) to first work this one out by himself.

My seventeen-year-old daughter is dating a much older guy

Q. *My daughter is seventeen years old and is in her final year at school. She is dating a guy who has just turned twenty-one. While her father and I don't agree with this, we're not sure how to go about telling her as we are afraid we will push her towards him even more if we tell her we don't want her seeing him. He is not from our area and we don't know much about him except that he works and, according to her, has a good job. She is very cautious when we ask for information about him. She seems to think that because he has done his Leaving Certificate and got six honours and has a good job, that's all that matters. But her dad and I are concerned about the age difference. As she is in her final year in school we want her to concentrate on her studies. She doesn't need any distraction as the guy is at a different stage in life. We have said if she was twenty-one and he was twenty-five it wouldn't matter as much because as you get older age levels out and the stages are more or less the same.*

A. A lot of parents would be worried about their teenage daughter going out with an older boyfriend and many of the concerns you have are valid. You do have a responsibility to ensure she is safe and not in a relationship she can't handle, as well as encouraging her to attend to her studies in her final year. However, at seventeen it is also important to support your daughter in making decisions about her own life and this is the balance you have to achieve.

SUPPORTING TEENAGERS IN MAKING IMPORTANT DECISIONS

As children become older teenagers, it is important to negotiate more with them and to reduce the number of blanket rules you have. This is especially the case about life decisions such as relationships and career choices, when your job as a parent is to prepare them to think through these issues themselves.

Rather than letting them suddenly make all decisions at age eighteen, the ideal is to start sooner, gradually giving them responsibility as they grow older. Indeed, eighteen is an arbitrary figure and some young people can make important decisions earlier, although most continue to benefit from their parents' guidance and support until much older.

BEING CLEAR ABOUT YOUR OWN VALUES

While the principle of gradually letting teenagers make their own decisions is a clear one, it is less clear at what age and what decisions to hand over. For example, at what age can your daughter or son have a boyfriend or girlfriend, or is it okay for a seventeen year old to have an older boyfriend when doing her Leaving Certificate?

These are individual family decisions that you have to work out for yourselves. A lot depends on your values as parents, what age you feel boyfriends are okay, and how much time you feel your daughter should spend studying, and so on.

UNDERSTANDING YOUR DAUGHTER

Much also depends on your daughter: some teenage girls are very responsible and can be trusted to have a boyfriend while also managing their studies. Other girls are less able to handle relationships and may need their parents to make a firmer decision. Some teenagers are even reassured when a parent makes a definite rule in this area, even though they may protest.

However, for other teenagers a blanket ban may not be effective and could even be counterproductive if it drives a wedge between you and your daughter and pushes her towards her boyfriend. So in deciding how to proceed you need to take a moment to reflect on your own values and also your daughter's needs and personality – then you can make a judgement call about what to do.

THE KEY IS COMMUNICATION

They key in all this is communication. It is great to see in your question that you are taking time to talk through all the issues with your daughter. Keep the lines of communication open and make sure to listen to her, as well as stating your own preferences. Take time to understand her point of view. Why is this relationship important to her? What does it mean to her? How important are her studies to her? How much support does she need with school work?

Try to respect and understand her choice of boyfriend – even if you have some reservations. Then also make sure to express your own concerns and issues: your worry about the age gap and whether she is able to handle this, your concern that she might be distracted from her studies, and so on. It is also important to discuss safety and sexuality in a frank and open way with her and to use the conversation to explore your worries and to help her think though the issues – how can she convince you she won't be exploited by him or how can she ensure she's not distracted from her studies?

Take plenty of time to communicate to see if you can find a win-win solution – a way forward that you are both happy with (for example, she sees him at certain times at the weekend and makes sure to work at her studies during the week). Or is there a workable compromise that she might reluctantly accept? For example, that she takes a break from the relationship until the exams are over and, in return, you provide her with rewards or incentives (weekend trips, etc.).

You can, of course, as a parent be definite about a rule in this area, but it is important to discuss it and try to reach an agreement and to take lots of time to communicate if your daughter feels strongly. Remember, though stressful, this dilemma represents an opportunity to deepen your relationship with your daughter as well as supporting her in thinking through issues and in learning to make responsible decisions for herself.

TECHNOLOGY AND SCREEN TIME

My teenagers are obsessed with technology

Q. *I have three children, aged sixteen, fourteen and eleven. My big question is what rules to set around using technology in the home. They seem to be always either watching TV, on the computer, using the Wii or texting friends. They're completely technology obsessed. They would spend the whole day on their devices if I let them. Sometimes I come in from work in the evening and all three of them are on a screen of some sort and it's hard to get a word out of them. Sometimes I get angry and insist everything is switched off but this just leads to a big row. What are reasonable expectations for teenagers these days?*

A. The question of how much to let technology into family life is an important one for parents today. Whereas in the 'old days' arguments focused on how much TV children and teenagers could watch, parents now have to contend with the internet, texting on mobile phones, tablets, computers and games consoles. Families are bombarded by technology and it can easily become an intrusion and interfere with family relationships. It is not just a problem for children and teenagers but also for parents who may be constantly checking emails at home or watching TV. Typical family scenes can involve one parent watching the TV and another on the computer, while the teenage children play games consoles, check social networking sites or text on mobile phones. Everyone is talking to someone else, and no one is talking to the people sitting beside them.

ENSURE YOU ARE IN CHARGE OF TECHNOLOGY AT HOME
While there are of course some benefits to all these new technologies in terms of leisure, learning and communication with the outside world, there are many disadvantages, such as distraction from active and healthy pursuits, interference with family relationships and stopping people being fully present at home. You can of course take steps as a parent to address this. The key is to make sure you are in charge of technology, rather than

technology being in charge of you. Rather than letting technology creep in and take over family life, you need to take a proactive stance and decide what role technology should have and set rules around this.

SET FAMILY RULES AROUND SCREEN TIME

Simple family rules around technology and screen time can make a big difference; for example, having no technology on in the mornings, stipulating that phones are left at the end of the table during mealtimes, 'switching off' all screens after a certain time in the evening, or having a technology-free evening at least once a week. It can also help to plan in advance when and where technology might be used. For example, you might agree with your teenagers that computer games can only be played after homework and for a limited amount of time. You could also agree on a few key programmes they want to watch on TV and stick to this to avoid aimless channel hopping or allowing technology to fill in all the gaps.

USE TECHNOLOGY TO ENHANCE FAMILY COMMUNICATION

When technology is allowed, try to make sure that it is beneficial and supports family communication. For example, you can join one of your teens searching on the internet as part of a school project or watch a favourite programme online together. Instead of criticising computer games, you could join in and use this as a source of shared fun as well as getting to know your teenager's specific interests. You could also organise a weekly family night when you have a shared meal and join together in 'screen time' by watching a favourite DVD, reviewing your favourite comedy scenes on YouTube, or playing a fitness game together on the Wii.

When I ask parents about when they discuss important issues with their teenagers, many say that they do so when it is brought up in the plot of a TV soap opera or documentary they are watching together. In these cases technology can be used as a means of communication rather than as a barrier. It is all about being tuned in and involved in what your children are doing.

NEGOTIATE CHANGES WITH YOUR TEENAGERS

Introducing changes in how technology is used in your family is likely to be resisted by your teenagers and it is important to set this up properly and to involve them in how it might be done. One creative way is to organise a family meeting (see Part 1, Step 9) with everyone present to raise your concerns about the overuse of technology and to listen to their views. It can help if you make it a family project to reflect together on how to make sure that technology is helpful for the family (perhaps you could search the subject together on the internet!). A lighthearted approach might also help – for example, you might set the challenge to see who can live without technology for a weekend (including the parents) and give a prize for who goes the longest. Take time as a family to think about this important issue and expect that it might take a few meetings or discussions before you decide what is best. While it is of course important that you take leadership in setting rules, the ideal is to empower your teenagers to reflect and make decisions about the issues themselves.

FOCUS ON HEALTHY PURSUITS

As well as setting rules on technology, it is also important to set goals around healthy family pursuits. According to some research, it is only when the use of technology interferes with a person's involvement in healthy activities such as sports, education, hobbies, social projects etc., that it becomes a problem. Even if your teens continue to spend a great deal of time using technology, as long as this is balanced by other healthy pursuits then it may not be such a problem. Such healthy pursuits can include family time, quality one-to-one time with parents and meaningful learning projects.

My thirteen-year-old wants to go on Facebook

Q. *Our eldest daughter just turned thirteen and is pushing to have a Facebook account. Her father and I are reluctant to let her do this, as you hear so many horror stories of cyberbullying and inappropriate usage etc. I'd prefer for her to wait until she is older but she accuses us of being old-fashioned and out of touch and argues that all her friends in school are on it. I have checked and this does seem to be the case, though she is one of the younger girls in the class. Because we didn't want her to be left out, we were prepared to allow her to have a Facebook account but only on the condition that we could know her password and thus could supervise what she is doing. She is dead set against this, saying none of her friends are supervised like this. I'm not sure what to do –what age should a child be allowed to use a social networking site? How can we keep her safe?*

A. As a parent you are right to be concerned about your daughter's online access and to take steps to supervise and to prepare her for using social networking websites such as Facebook. It is hard to recommend a specific age as a lot depends on your child's maturity and the context in which she will be online. In addition, access to the internet is increasing at a huge rate and children are accessing websites at younger and younger ages. This has educational benefits as well as potential risks and dangers. Facebook set a guide that children should be at least thirteen before they use the site, though this is not policed and it is clear that much younger children are using it regularly. In a large European study published in 2011 (EU Kids Online), it was found that 20 per cent of nine to twelve-year-olds had a Facebook profile and this rose to 46 per cent for thirteen-to-sixteen-year-olds. However, it is up to you to decide what is best for your daughter. The following guidelines might help:

BE PREPARED TO SET RULES ABOUT ONLINE USE
During the early teenage years, children often push for independence and believe they can handle much more than they actually can, which makes it particularly important for parents to set boundaries and to be there to supervise. Don't worry about bucking the trend or appearing old-fashioned – the best parents are often conservative and cautious. Certainly, setting rules with a teenager is unlikely to win you a popularity contest. It is perfectly reasonably for you to delay her starting on Facebook until you think she is ready and/or to set a condition that she must add you as a friend when she does get an account or that she must review all new friend requests with you first.

BE PREPARED TO NEGOTIATE

It is also important to listen carefully to your daughter's point of view and to understand what it means for her to join a social networking site. Ultimately you want to try to find a win-win, or at least show her a future pathway that allows her to get what she wants once you are sure she has learned how to be safe. Sometimes teenagers want to go on social networking sites so they can connect with friends they don't see often – as an alternative to going online you could make an extra effort to facilitate her meeting these friends via trips or by inviting them for sleepovers etc.

GRADUALLY INCREASE HER INDEPENDENCE

Rather than giving your daughter full freedom and access to the internet, often the best approach is a gradual one. Set a date in the future when she can start using Facebook and then set conditions, such as she has to go through a safety lesson online with you before she starts and that initially you have a login and password for her page also. You can reassure her that once she shows she can be safe and gets to grips with how it all works you will give her more privacy and independence as she earns your trust.

TAKE TIME TO TEACH HER ONLINE SAFETY

Use her request to go online as an opportunity teach her about online safety and responsibility. Discuss the rule about not giving any personal information out online and how she might respond if approached by unknown people. Make sure to discuss cyberbullying with her, advising her to be both careful what she says about people (as others can read it) and also making sure she tells you if someone posts hurtful stuff about other people. Use this safety discussion as an opportunity to learn together about the internet (e.g. logging on to a sample account together or visiting many of the good educational websites on internet safety for teens such as www.webwise.ie). Done well, this could be a chance for you to begin to discuss some important life issues with her and to learn about her opinions and point of view.

SET A LIMIT ON SCREEN TIME IN THE HOME

Many teens become obsessed with using the internet in general and social networking sites in particular. It is important that you set limits on the amount of internet use or screen time in the household and make sure that time spent online is not to the detriment of other social and active pursuits. This can include setting a limit on screen time, such as one hour a day, only after homework is done, not after 8 p.m. or only in family spaces. It can be helpful for the whole family to have regular technology-free times, such as during meals. If this feels hard to establish you can start by having a special family night once a week when technology is banned and everyone returns to the traditional mode of simple conversation and face-to-face communication.

My seventeen-year-old has been viewing pornography on his phone

Q. *We bought our seventeen-year-old son a smartphone five months ago for his birthday. He had been pressing to get one for ages, 'like all his friends', and we finally gave in. He was out the other day and forgot to take his phone with him, which is unusual as it is normally welded to him. I took the opportunity to look at it. I know I shouldn't have, but I was curious to see what he was up to on it. Looking at his history and apps I discovered he was regularly accessing porn and adult sites. As his mother, I was shocked. I know that you should expect this from teenagers, but I didn't like it at all, especially as some of the sites were vile and give a distorted view on sexuality. I don't know what to do. Should I raise it with him? I would feel embarrassed about this. How much of it is a problem? My husband thinks it is a case of 'boys will be boys' but I am not so sure.*

A. Despite the clear communication and educational potential of the internet, a big side-effect has been the increased access to and usage of pornography. With the advent of smartphones, this access has increased further, meaning people can potentially be online twenty-four hours a day.

There is evidence that teenagers are now accessing pornography at earlier ages and more frequently than previous generations.

As a parent you are right to be worried about this trend. While there can be an attitude of bravado, that it is no harm and that 'boys will be boys' (although girls are now also accessing similar sites), there is a genuine concern as to how this increased exposure will affect teenagers and their expectations of adult relationships.

As a society, we are not yet sure what impact growing up in the age of the internet has, with young people spending increasing amounts of time online and access to pornography and other explicit material always just a click away. Part of the problem is the potentially addictive nature both of spending time online and of viewing pornography in particular, which can lead to some teenagers being isolated and suffering from poor self-esteem.

EMPOWERING YOUR TEENAGER

Whereas with children and younger teenagers you can adopt a strict vigilance stance and take steps such as supervising their usage, installing filtering on family PCs or restricting the internet on their phones, this is less appropriate with older teenagers who have a right to a degree of privacy and independence. In addition, it is hard to find software on PCs that block all inappropriate sites or software that a technology-savvy teenager can't bypass if they want to.

The problem is even harder on smartphones. You can check history and supervise usage, but a teenager can easily hide what they are doing or view pornography elsewhere. With older teenagers, supervision can go only so far. What is more important is to try to talk through the issues with your teenagers and to encourage them to self-regulate their usage.

In the long term, you want them to make informed choices about what they view on the internet and to develop their own discipline about this.

A DELICATE CONVERSATION

Raising this conversation with a teenager is a delicate matter and it is important to pick a good time. Probably the best thing is to raise the issue directly and in a matter-of-fact way by explaining you discovered the porn on his phone and you want to discuss with him whether it is appropriate. Be prepared for the fact that he is likely to initially get embarrassed or defensive about the subject, but take time to listen to what he thinks and feels about it. Try not to be too judgemental and acknowledge that it is normal to have a curiosity about viewing sexually explicit material.

Then explain your concerns about the material (for example, how it presents a distorted view of relationships). Given his age, it can work best if you state your opinion rather than categorical rules, such as, 'I'd prefer you not to look at this material on the internet' or 'I hope you don't think that this is how real relationships work' or 'As a woman, I find this material offensive' and so on, depending on your own views.

Although it is a delicate conversation, it could open a useful dialogue with your son and he may even take on board some of your concerns. You can consider setting some limits on the use of his phone (by turning off the wireless at night or blocking inappropriate sites, for example) but ideally you should aim to get him on board and agree to these as part of his self-discipline.

INCLUDE THE OTHER PARENT IN THE CONVERSATION

If possible, it is best if both you and his father talk to him about the issue and this is probably best done as two separate conversations. You can present your opinion as his mother and give the perspective of a woman, and his father can empathise with what he is going through as a young man. If you feel uncomfortable about the conversation you could ask his father to start the conversation with him.

CONSIDER SEEKING SUPPORT IF NEEDED

While for most teenagers viewing pornography is infrequent and not a problem, for some it is excessive and may be addictive. When you talk to your son, if you get a sense that it is a more significant problem for him, do seek help from addiction services who should be able to give you more specific advice.

SETTING RULES AND DEALING WITH DIFFICULT BEHAVIOUR

Our thirteen-year-old son has got a constant attitude towards us

Q. *Our thirteen-year-old son has become very difficult recently. He is displaying a constant attitude in the way he talks to us, and acts as if this is a 'cool' way to behave. He is also challenging all our rules, saying none of his friends have the same rules. For example, we have told him he can't go to town until he is fifteen, but he says all his friends go now. My question is how can we discipline him when his friends don't have the same rules and how can we deal with his attitude?*

A. Parenting a young teenager can be hard work and reaching the age of thirteen can bring particular challenges. As a parent, it can be a real shock as your previously easy-going child starts pushing the boundaries and appears to develop an attitude overnight. Though it is hard to cope with, you are not alone and what you are dealing with is relatively normal.

In responding to this challenging time, the key as a parent is to separate the important rules from the negotiable ones. It comes with the territory for teenagers to question their parents' authority, to seek more independence, to seek the company of their peers more and to become more private. These changes are all part and parcel of growing up and are even healthy for your teenager as they forge their own identity.

INSIST ON RESPECT

However, this quest for independence does not have to be done with an attitude – teenagers should continue to respect their parents and this is important for them (in learning how to deal with authority) as well as important to parents (who deserve to be dealt with respectfully).

In fact, insisting on the rule of respect is probably the most important principle to maintain when you are parenting a teenager. This means that if your teen talks to you with contempt or aggression, you calmly pause the conversation and say, 'Hold on, I can't talk to you until you speak politely' or 'Take a moment, we can only talk when you are calm.'

This principle of respect works both ways and you must commit to always speaking respectfully to your teenager – what you do and how you behave is more important than what you say.

NEGOTIATE RULES AS MUCH AS POSSIBLE

It is important to be prepared to negotiate and talk through rules with teenagers in a much more explicit manner than you might with a younger child. While you still make the final decision, it is important to recognise that soon they will be making these decisions themselves, so you need to plan to hand over the responsibility for this. Done respectfully, you can use the process of conversation and negotiation as a means to teach your teen about safety and allow him to gradually take on responsibility.

When your son asks to go into town with his friends, you might encourage him to talk more about what he wants – where does he want to go, which friends does he plan to go with, why is it important to go, and so on. Use this as an opportunity to listen and to hear about what is important to him. Then explain your concerns and reservations.

When doing this it is important to express them in terms of positive values or principles that are in his interest. For example, 'As a parent I need to know you are safe, I need to be sure you are ready to go into town.' Then be prepared to explore possible solutions and ways forward with questions such as, 'How can you ensure you will be safe in town?' and to examine hypothetical dangers by asking, 'How would you deal with [a particular occurrence] if it happened?' The goal is to try to reach a win-win agreement whereby you find a way forward that both gives your teen some legitimate steps to independence, while also allowing you to be fully reassured of his safety.

Even if this is not possible, you can negotiate compromises or alternatives such as, 'You can go if we collect you, or only if you go with [a friend you trust] or only if you're home before 6 p.m.'

You can, of course, say no to the whole idea, but try to present this positively and explain under what future conditions you could change your mind – for example, 'You can go when you are fourteen.' It is also okay to kick for touch and to decide later: 'I'll talk to some of the other parents [of the friends] and see what they think', and so on.

ENCOURAGE HIS INDEPENDENCE STEP BY STEP

Rather than either saying no or giving your teen everything he wants, it can be useful to break the request into smaller increments, whereby he gains your trust step by step. For example, 'If you can come in on time as agreed each evening this week then we can look at you going out for a short time at the weekend.'

If at any point the conversation becomes disrespectful it is important to take a pause. Always make an agreement conditional on respect: 'Until you talk politely, we won't be able to agree to you going out at all.' You may have to back this up with consequences and loss of privileges.

SHOWING YOUR SON HOW TO COMMUNICATE

While there aren't any absolute rules for teenagers, there are principles for respectfully talking through boundaries and this is the key to successful parenting. While there may not be a definite age when a teenager is responsible enough to go into town unsupervised (a lot depends on how mature or able he is, how responsible his friends are, and your own cultural values as a family), it is important to consider the issue carefully and to talk it through with your teenager.

Done well, such negotiations provide a good model for teenagers in how to communicate effectively and can deepen your relationship with them as they grow up.

My teen's tantrums are disrupting family life

Q. *To what extent can hormone changes affect a teenager's behaviour and mood? I have a fifteen-year-old son who, all in all, is very good in terms of his behaviour. However, he is almost six-feet tall and his voice has broken, so when he is in a bad mood, his presence and mood are felt by the whole family. When he is angry or annoyed over something that he is not allowed to do, he raises his voice and ends up shouting. Every time he shouts, we ask him to lower his voice and to speak respectfully if the conversation is to* *continue. But his reactions have a negative effect on the atmosphere in the house and on other family members. We have discussed this with him, so he is aware of how he is affecting others, but on the days he is in a bad mood, he forgets all this. This can be quite disheartening for us as parents – sometimes I don't recognise my son in the grumpy/moody young man in front of me. If he so wanted, he could make life very difficult for us at home – fortunately he doesn't go that far but, to be honest, given his size I feel that there is nothing stopping him from ultimately doing what he wants. I know that we can hold back on money and other things he may want, but when he is in a mood, those things don't seem to matter too much to him. I think as a parent, I would feel more reassured if I had some idea to what extent the moods are just part of being a teenager and will pass. There are days when my son is a pleasure to live with; those days are great and he is more content himself. A small child may have a tantrum and a parent can deal with it, but a six-foot teenager with a man's voice having a tantrum is a much more difficult situation to manage while trying to maintain some element of harmony in the family home. What are your views on and experience of this with teenage boys?*

A. What you describe is a very common experience for parents of teenagers. Teenagers can become very challenging and disrespectful, and their physical size can make these rows much more intimidating than when they were younger. You ask about whether hormones are a significant factor in these changes and the short answer is yes, definitely!

One of the reasons for the deterioration in many children's behaviour when they become teenagers is the physical and developmental changes they go through. With a physical growth spurt, their bodies experience tremendous changes. They can experience much stronger and more intense emotions, can be more critical and challenging intellectually and can feel more pressure within peer groups and school.

In addition, these changes all come at a time when developmentally they are pushing for independence from the family, and a normal part of this is being critical and negative towards their parents while valuing peers and role models outside the family. All this is a recipe for conflict.

The good news is that this phase does tend to pass. Most of the families I work with describe having a 'bad year' with one of their teenagers before things begin to improve or settle. As a result, hanging in there and putting things in perspective are important.

BE SYMPATHETIC TO YOUR SON, BUT ALSO INSIST ON RESPECT

In terms of managing the situation, the best approach is a balance between being sympathetic to what your son is going through and standing up to his disrespectful behaviour. With teenagers, often the problem is not what they are saying but how they are saying it. It is perfectly legitimate for them to question rules and to ask for more independence, though it is not okay for them to intimidate people or make the family suffer their bad mood.

Discipline does have a part to play also. It is important that you have a good plan of action as to how you will respond when he reacts angrily. Usually, the best advice is to first request that he speak respectfully, but if he fails to do so, to tactfully interrupt the discussion until he calms down.

Your own emotional response is key at these times. If you let his anger intimidate you or you get angry in return, this can make matters worse. This is hard to do and is the reason I suggest that parents use consequences rather than criticising or haranguing their teen to behave. Examples of effective consequences are a loss of pocket money, reduced TV time or, most effectively, a delay of his original request (for example, 'Because you shouted, you will now have to wait a half hour before I drive you to your friend's house').

You are correct that a warning of consequences may not work immediately, but the key is following up with them. A follow-up conversation with your son when he is calmer is probably the most important aspect of this process. During this conversation, you need to share with him the impact of his moods on everyone and to remind him that his privileges in the house are dependent on respectful behaviour.

REMAIN POSITIVE

It is also important to be positive with him (for example, 'Come on, you normally behave so well'), as well as to get his take on what happened and to talk through strategies to manage his anger, such as pausing and taking a deep breath. Even if he forgets all of this in the moment, it is important to persist with these conversations and to keep putting it back to him to think of solutions – 'What can you do to make sure you don't get into these arguments?' Ultimately, the goal is to help him learn how to manage his anger and moods and over time to show him how to communicate more effectively.

My eighteen-year-old daughter is becoming violent and angry

Q. *My eighteen-year-old daughter is always angry and sometimes in a rage. At the moment I am sweeping up broken glass from the door she kicked in. She is becoming increasingly violent and it is frightening me. My husband wants her to leave the house. What can I do to manage this situation and where can I go to get her help (I lost my job so can't afford much)?*

A. Though it is not often talked about, many parents experience ongoing bullying and violent behaviour from their children and teenagers, which can range from verbal abuse and threats to the destruction of property and even physical violence. Whereas this can be easier to deal with when children are young, it becomes much more alarming as they become older, when the behaviour can be more extreme and intimidating.

UNDERSTANDING AGGRESSIVE BEHAVIOUR
There are many reasons for such behaviour and often no one cause: sometimes it is brought on by underlying problems such as drinking, drug taking or being in a delinquent peer group. It is more common in families in which the child has witnessed similar behaviour from parents or family members. Frequently, it is a pattern of behaviour which started as a means of getting their own way as a young child and escalates as they get older.

The first step to dealing with violent or bullying behaviour is to decide that it is unacceptable and needs to be addressed. This may seem obvious, but some parents collude with their children's behaviour by feeling guilty for past family events (perhaps where the child witnessed violence) or by thinking their child has an underlying problem which makes it hard for them to control themselves (such as Attention Deficit Hyperactivity Disorder or Conduct Disorder). Remember that even if your child has such a history or diagnosis, violent behaviour is still unacceptable and you must address it. You do your children no favours by allowing them to disrespect or abuse you.

TALK TO YOUR DAUGHTER REGARDING HER BEHAVIOUR

The next step is to sit down and explain to your daughter that you will not tolerate aggression at home. The key is to focus on the importance of respect as the primary rule of the house rather than other less important issues (such as cleaning their room etc.).

You then need to think through what consequences you will need to enforce when the problem arises. Like your husband, many parents in these circumstances consider insisting their child leaves the home if another violent incident occurs. However, you may be reluctant to do this as you might worry that it will damage your relationship or will leave her exposed to extra dangers if she lives away.

THINK THROUGH CONSEQUENCES FOR HER BEHAVIOUR

I suggest you keep the option of her leaving home as your last resort, and that you explore less severe consequences as your first port of call. Make a list of all the privileges your daughter gains by living at home such as laundry, cooked meals, access to a phone, using the car, money and a private bedroom. Then make these dependent on her behaving respectfully. If she gets abusive, then remove one of these privileges as a consequence.

What works varies from teenager to teenager, but it is important to make the consequence as small as possible so the teenager can work to have the privilege restored – by showing remorse or trying to be respectful.

EXAMINE YOUR OWN RESPONSES TO HER OUTBURSTS

You need to examine your own reactions to the violent incidents. For example, many parents inadvertently fuel the escalation of a row by nagging or lecturing, or using threats and physical discipline themselves. The key is to commit to a calm, firm and non-violent approach. When dealing with a row that could escalate into an aggressive incident, it is important to interrupt these patterns early. The minute your daughter becomes abusive you need to pause and interrupt the row – 'I'm not going to talk to you until you speak politely to me' – and warn your child of a consequence either then or later.

Of course, this can be difficult to do, especially if you feel intimidated or scared. This is why it is important to seek support. It can really help if you and your husband work together in this calm and firm approach. Decide on a back-up plan if you are dealing with an incident alone – such as calling a neighbour or friend, or even the police if an incident gets out of hand (you can contact the police in advance to discuss how they might help).

Once you get through an incident, you must later talk through what happened with your daughter, making sure to impose a consequence (such as paying for the damage) and exploring with her how she can be respectful the next time. This follow-up is crucial in order to help her take responsibility.

REACH OUT TO YOUR DAUGHTER

As well as being firm in dealing with the aggression, it is important to try to reach out to her and to understand what is going on for her. You can be sympathetic to the problems and stresses that might be in her life (perhaps lack of work, relationship problems or other issues), though they are not an excuse for bad behaviour. While things may be under strain at the moment, it can help to try and improve your relationship with her. The more you can have times of ordinary chat, the easier it will be to get along and this will reduce the likelihood of problems. Make a list of things you might connect on. When did you last have an enjoyable conversation? Perhaps it was when you went for a walk or did something you liked together. Think of ways you can increase these shared happy experiences.

CONSIDER GETTING PROFESSIONAL SUPPORT

Finally, seek professional support. It is difficult to deal with violence alone and professional services might help. In the first instance, contact Parentline

(1890 927 277), which can provide support and suggest services in your area. There are also good international websites on dealing with teenage violence such as www.parentlink.act.gov.au and www.eddiegallagher.id.au.

How can I stick to the rules with my teenager?

Q. *One of the difficulties I have with my fourteen-year-old daughter is sticking to what I say. For example, my daughter did something that I was clear about her not being allowed to do. So I told her she was grounded for the week. After two days of being grounded she said she was sorry and had learned her lesson (there just happened to be a party she wanted to go to the next day). She then went on to explain why I should allow her to get off being grounded – and, to tell the truth, it was really logical. So after an internal struggle I said okay. I am proud of her, and who she is developing into, but as it is my job to teach her, and I'm a single parent, I just wonder what happens next time? Should I have stood my ground? Sometimes I feel like she can just wear me down and I cave in. Also, it would be great to get some guidance, words or directions on how to communicate to teens in a way they understand; like, how do you reason with them? I don't want to control her, but I want her to understand why I say some of the things I do, and saying she will understand when she gets older isn't working for either of us.*

A. Your question raises some of the particular challenges of parenting teenagers. The early teenage years are often marked by a push for independence and increased conflict with parents over rules and boundaries. In addition, teenagers can become more sophisticated in how they argue and negotiate, and frequently they make valid arguments to their parents that cause them to rethink their position.

As a result, it is easy to become confused as to how to respond. On the one hand, you want to encourage your teen's good negotiation and recognise their legitimate need for more freedom but, on the other hand, you don't want to give in or feel undermined or bullied by your teenager.

BE CLEAR ABOUT YOUR NON-NEGOTIABLE RULES

In moving forward, the first step is to become clear in your own mind as to what is negotiable and what is non-negotiable with your teenager. Or put another way, what are the core rules that you need to hold as a parent in order to facilitate your teenager growing up well and to maintain harmony in the home? Usually, I suggest parents keep these core rules to a minimum, centred on important things such as safety, health, education and respect.

If any rule does not come under any of these areas, then it is largely negotiable or up to the teen to decide for themselves. Indeed you want to encourage teens to negotiate and to be able to make their own decisions – these are key life skills you want to help them learn. The key rule to enforce with teenagers is respect. You want them to learn to negotiate their point respectfully.

IT IS NOT OKAY FOR YOUR TEEN TO BADGER YOU

How teenagers communicate is often as important as what they are communicating. It is okay for them to push for freedom and to question rules, but it is not okay for them to over-argue, badger or bully you.

In your own example, when your daughter was negotiating about going out again, if you felt she was being reasonable and respectful, then it is perfectly okay for you to relax the rule and give her another chance. Indeed, you can point out to her that you are trusting her with another chance and that you expect her to continue to behave well to earn this privilege.

However, if you feel she is arguing her point negatively or trying to pull a fast one, then it is important for you to hold your ground and to address her lack of respect. You can remind her that the only way she will make progress is by being honest and speaking to you respectfully.

FIND CONSEQUENCES THAT WILL WORK WITH YOUR DAUGHTER

Your question also highlights the importance of thinking through your consequences in advance. As well as advising parents to keep their rules to a minimum, I also advise them to keep their consequences as small as possible. For example, in the future you could ground her for one or two days rather than a week, which is easier for you to enforce and makes it less likely that you are put in the position of having to back down.

Rather than using a big consequence, it is more useful to employ a small one that your daughter is likely to keep, which then reinforces your authority, rather than one that is too large and too difficult to enforce. In some cases, it can work better to put a condition on the consequence rather than a fixed length of time. For example, you could have said that she has to stay in until she talks politely to you about what happened or persuades you that she can be trusted once again.

PROBLEM SOLVING WITH YOUR DAUGHTER

You also ask in your question how best to communicate with teens about rules so they take on board what you are saying. The first principle is to always listen first and to make sure to understand what is important for your teen. Then you can state your own concerns directly and clearly. Present them in a way that benefits your teenager rather than as a statement of your authority. For example, statements of good rules include, 'I am only insisting you are collected so I know you are safe and well' or 'As your mother I need to know where you are going or who you are with.'

Finally, in disputes over rules with teenagers it helps if, as much as possible, you can try to find a win-win. For example, you want to find a way for your teen to get what they want or need, within the context of keeping the important rules. For example, how can they get out to meet their friends in a way that you feel they are safe and secure?

Win-win solutions might include accompanying them to and from venues, inviting their friends over, making contact with their friends' parents or any other number of ideas that work for both of you.

FAMILY RELATIONSHIPS

My sixteen- and fifteen-year-old girls are always competing and bickering

Q. *My sixteen-year-old daughter has always been a strong character and a bit fiery, but recently she seems to be fighting with everyone. She is very competitive and always trying to pick fights, particularly with her younger sister, who is a much more laid-back character. They are very close in age, just one year between them, and I think a lot of the conflict stems from jealousy. My younger daughter has started to do well in school and our eldest is very competitive and puts her down. It has got to a point where we can't praise the youngest if she gets a good report or else the older girl will throw a tantrum. Don't get me wrong, we try not to compare them and always try to be positive towards both of them. But, to be honest, because the older girl is so negative and always in trouble this has become a lot harder recently.*

A. Jealousy and rivalry between siblings is very common and a significant factor in many family conflicts, particularly when one child is unhappy or 'acting out'. Furthermore, sibling rivalry can become particularly acute during adolescence when teenagers are trying to work out their individual identity and what they stand for as distinct from other people in the family. At this time you may also be dealing as parents with teenage rebellion, which can make it a fraught time for everyone in the family.

UNDERSTANDING SIBLING RIVALRY AND COMPETITIVENESS

At the heart of sibling rivalry is a fight for parents' approval and attention. Children and teenagers frequently fear that their parents might approve or love one sibling more than another, or that their parents' approval is dependent on a certain quality or skill that their sibling might have more of. While, of course, as parents you strive to love each of your children equally and not to pit them against each other, much of the competitive pressure comes from outside the home. The educational system and many sporting disciplines emphasise attainment that distinguishes who is 'the best'. This can be particularly difficult for teenagers if they are not performing as well as their brother or sister in these arenas and can lead to conflict and poor self-esteem.

SIBLING RIVALRY CAN BE INADVERTENTLY REINFORCED BY PARENTS' REACTIONS

Without meaning to, your reactions as parents can reinforce sibling rivalry. For example, any time you praise your youngest in front of the eldest (particularly around exam achievement if this is a sensitive issue) this can make her feel more insecure and even believe that you favour the younger girl.

In addition, if during an argument you intervene on the side of one of your girls, this can leave the other feeling you favour her sister. This happens even when you intervene for a good reason, such as when your eldest daughter might appear to be in the wrong or shouts at her sister.

PRAISE AND ENCOURAGE THEM EQUALLY AND UNIQUELY

To counter this you need to go out of your way to make sure you provide your two daughters with equal amounts of attention and encouragement. You should also avoid praise that somehow makes a comparison or implies a criticism of the other. As it is a sensitive issue, this might mean not praising your youngest for her education grades in front of the eldest for the moment. Instead, you might want to emphasise more non-comparable qualities such as 'doing your best' or 'being proud of your hard work'. When praising the two of them you should emphasise qualities that both girls can aspire to as well as any shared strengths and interests that might bring them together.

It is also important to encourage each of their unique and individual qualities (e.g. if one has a passion for music and the other for art) that allow them to appreciate each other differently without competition. You want each girl to find their niche and place in life as distinct from the other.

EMPOWER THEM TO SORT OUT THEIR OWN DISPUTES

In addition, it is important not to take sides in any disputes or rows they might have but rather to empower them to sort out these disputes themselves. Your role is not to judge who is wrong but rather to be a mediator and to help them both work out how to manage things. If you do need to intervene, try to address both of them – 'Let's take a moment for both of you to calm down and talk this out.' And if you do need to correct them, make sure you hold them both accountable at some level. For example, you might say to the eldest, 'You should try to explain your point without shouting', and to the youngest: 'You should listen to your sister without rolling your eyes.'

HELP THEM EMPATHISE WITH EACH OTHER

When talking to your daughters individually about problems, never judge the other and always help them empathise with their sister. For example, you might explain privately to the youngest that her sister is sensitive to a big deal being made of exam results and explain to the oldest that her younger sister finds loud conflicts hard to deal with. You want to communicate that you understand both of them individually and that you are on both their sides in sorting things out.

TAKE STEPS TO SUPPORT THEIR RELATIONSHIP WITH EACH OTHER

Do what you can to help them spend time together and to enjoy each other's company. Simple things like sending them on a shopping trip together to buy something for the family or putting them on the same team in a family game could help. You could also help them learn to get on by setting them a task such as organising a family celebration or decorating a room together, for which they might earn a reward if they work as a team.

Once they become less competitive in seeking your approval and more secure in their relationship with each other, you would expect them to be able to enjoy the other's successes and to become close, supportive sisters as they grow up.

My teenagers don't talk to each other

Q. *I am a father of three teenage children – a girl of fourteen and two boys, aged sixteen and nineteen. The problem is that there is no communication between them. It is not that they row, just not much communication. It seems as if they are living separate lives without talking to one another. This has been going on for a long time – maybe four years or more – and it went unnoticed for quite a while. I can't identify a particular starting point or cause of the problem. The last time I remember things being better was when the eldest started secondary school nearly seven years ago. He would chat to his brother about school and I used to have to stop them talking to get them to sleep. Now I wish I could have that back as there just isn't any talk unless I tell one of them to go tell the other dinner is ready, or whatever, and that's it. Now and then I do ask them to make an effort to talk and they say they will, but nothing has changed. I should say that when I was growing up communication was poor in my family, though my brother and sister and I get on very well today. I wonder at times if this is where the problem might come from, though my brother and sister don't have the same problem with their kids. I feel it's very unhealthy and I worry how much longer this situation will continue. I feel my children are missing out and, at times, I become stressed about this issue.*

A. During adolescence, lots of teenagers become private and begin to disconnect from their family – this is part of the process of growing up. For some, this extends to siblings and it is common for teenagers to pull away from their brothers and sisters for a period and for their friends and peer group to become more important in their lives. Just as it is normal for parents to get upset at their teenager pulling away from them, it is also normal to be worried at their changing relationship with brothers and sisters.

TEENAGERS' RELATIONSHIPS WITH SIBLINGS

Lots of parents have an expectation of their children being close and having good relationships when they grow up and can be disappointed if this is not the case. If close sibling bonds endure into adulthood, parents feel reassured that their children will be happier and looked out for as adults.

It could be that your children's current lack of communication is simply a feature of being teenagers and it is not necessarily an indication that they won't be close as adults. Indeed, you describe how you were not close to your siblings growing up, yet now you communicate well with them as adults.

It is worth reflecting as to how and when your relationships with your siblings improved. Were there specific events that brought you closer or was it that you all simply grew up and learned to talk more? This might give you some clues as to how your own children's relationships might change and what you can do to facilitate them.

HELPING YOUR TEENAGERS COMMUNICATE BETTER WITH EACH OTHER

How you can help your children communicate better depends on a variety of things. For example, do they actively avoid each other or do they simply not currently share any interests or activities? Do they talk more in different contexts, such as when they're out of the house or doing something they enjoy? Depending on the answers to these questions, perhaps you could help them communicate more by setting a routine in the house around shared meals or family events, or you could build upon any shared interests they have (e.g. by paying for two of them to go to a football match together if it interests them both). Alternatively, you could encourage them to undertake some tasks together (maybe a joint household project that you might reward them for on completion, such as painting a room).

Depending on the situation, you could also look for opportunities to set up one sibling in a helping role with another – maybe the eldest might be in a position to help the youngest with homework and this could work if both were open to it and it fitted with their personalities.

FOCUS ON YOUR OWN RELATIONSHIP WITH EACH OF THEM INDIVIDUALLY

I'm also interested to know how you and their mother get on with them individually. How close are your relationships with each of them? This is certainly something to work on by making time to chat and listen to each of them one-to-one, and setting up shared interests and tasks together.

Aside from being good for you both independently, it is during these one-to-ones that they might discuss their relationship with their brothers or sister and, if your relationship is close, you are then best placed to support and positively influence them. Certainly, the best time to help is when one of them raises the issue directly with you. They might not do this until a later time, but you should be ready to respond.

TAKING A LONG-TERM VIEW

However, it could also be that the best approach is to take a step back and to wait for them to sort out their own relationships themselves. Certainly, putting them under any pressure might be counterproductive and you might be best taking a long-term view and waiting for things to improve naturally as they did in your own family.

In summary, focus on building your own individual relationship with each of your teenagers, and then look for subtle or indirect opportunities to encourage them to talk with one another. Ideally, wait for one of them to raise the issue with you as this is when they are most likely to listen and take on board your suggestions.

My son blames me for the separation

Q. *I separated from my husband just under two years ago, mainly due to his drinking and gambling. It has been a hard couple of years though things are a lot better now. My ex has got his act together. He lives with his mother, has stopped drinking and gambling and sees the children regularly. The problem is my oldest son, who turned thirteen last month. He has become really cheeky and disrespectful to me at home. He has been critical of me and everything I do. In particular, he doesn't like me going out to socialise and makes negative comments that I am 'too old' to go out, etc. It's weird but it reminds me of the way that his dad used to try to control me during the bad times. I thought a lot of the problems were his age and teen hormones but then we had a big row last weekend and he blurted out that he didn't know* *why I 'threw Dad out of the house'. I saw red and blew my top at him. I was furious to be blamed for what was really all his dad's fault. Now I feel guilty for shouting at him and I am also really annoyed at his dad who seems to be having conversations with my son which somehow make him out to be the innocent party. What should I do?*

A. PARENTAL SEPARATION AND ADOLESCENCE

Parenting an adolescent can have its ups and downs at the best of times and in the context of parental separation it can bring special challenges. During the adolescent years children can reexperience some of the hurt and confusion they might have originally felt about their parents' separation. As they can now think in more complicated ways, new questions can emerge for them as to why their parents separated, and they can feel a divided sense of loyalty more acutely than before. Frequently, to make sense of what happened, they can feel they have to take a side or judge one of their parents for being at fault for the separation.

TEENAGERS' DISCOMFORT WITH PARENTS' NEW RELATIONSHIPS

As they are dealing with their own emerging sexuality, adolescents can be uncomfortable with their parents starting new relationships. This could be the source of your son's criticism of your socialising. While, of course, you can appreciate his upset and confusion, it is not okay for him to be disrespectful or aggressive towards you. While you can understand some of his discomfort about you dating, it is not acceptable for him to try to control your life or to feel he can negatively comment about your social life.

To help him, the key is to encourage him to express his feelings, worries and upset, but in a way that is respectful to both you and his father. At thirteen he probably needs more information about the separation; indeed teenagers appreciate being spoken to in a more adult way about the circumstances of the separation as they become more able to understand.

RAISE THE ISSUE OF THE SEPARATION WITH YOUR SON

Use the fact that you had a row as an opportunity to approach him at a better time to raise the subject of the separation. Pick a time when he

is calm and open and check in with how he is feeling: 'I am sorry we had a row the other day, but you raised some important worries about how your dad and I separated.' Try to listen without judgement to what he says and encourage him to share his feelings. When you do explain the circumstances of the separation to him, try to do this in a way that is factual and does not blame either you or his father or that is at least compassionate to you both.

If you can, it is a good idea to first present your perspective on how the marriage ended and then to also try to give his father's perspective. You can have different views but that is all right. During this conversation you can emphasise the importance of respect and remind your son of the importance of respecting you whatever his feelings.

INVOLVING HIS FATHER IN THE DISCUSSION

If possible, the ideal is for this information to come from both you and his father. You don't say how communication is between you and your ex at the moment, but it is important to tell him about what happened and to seek his support in resolving things.

As well as your son having individual conversations with you and his father about the separation, it might be useful if the three of you could sit down and go over things together, at least initially. That way your son will see you working together as parents and will feel less pressure to judge or to take a side.

Finally, remember that your son is starting his teen years which can be a bumpy ride for child and parents alike. Though he might be pulling away, think of how you can stay connected with him. Prioritise and build on the times when you do get on well with him, whether this is chats before bed, going for a walk or even watching a favourite TV programme together.

For more information, please see *When Parents Separate: Helping your Children Cope* (see Further Reading for full details).

My daughter won't accept discipline from my new partner

Q. *I was a single mother for many years and then met a new partner four years ago. I have a thirteen-year-old daughter who was nine when she first met my partner. My partner has always been wonderful with my daughter and they get on great as a rule. However, she does not accept discipline from him and this causes lots of conflict, particularly since she became a teen. Do you have any guidance on how I should manage this?*

A. Introducing a new partner to your children and creating a new family unit is a complex process at the best of times. Everyone is faced with the challenge of working out their new relationships with each other.

BECOMING A STEP-PARENT: A SPECIAL RELATIONSHIP

Your partner must deal with the challenge of forming a relationship with your daughter and working out how much of a stepfather role he should adopt. You are faced with the challenge of moving from being a single parent, when there were just the two of you, to including your partner in the family and balancing your relationship with both of them.

While things can often go very well, there can be conflict, particularly if you have different expectations of each of the relationships and how people should fit in. For example, whereas you may expect that your partner would be able to adopt a stepfather role in your daughter's life, this may not be the way she sees things. She might see your partner as simply your companion and not expect him to be a father to her.

Your daughter was relatively old when your partner was introduced to her and though she might see him as supportive or even a fun person in her life, she might not expect him to adopt a parental role, particularly around discipline. In addition, although she might get on with him most of the time, she might also feel rivalry towards him – after all, she had you to herself for many years and now she has to share your attention.

YOUR DAUGHTER IS WORKING OUT HER IDENTITY

Though you don't mention any details, another factor is whether your daughter has or has had a relationship with her birth father, her perception of him and the circumstances in which you became a single parent. All these issues can come to a head when children hit the teenage years. At age thirteen it is very normal for children to begin to separate and pull away from their parents. They begin to question their parents' rules and start a journey towards independence and making their own decisions.

As parents you can experience this as conflict because your rules and values are challenged and it can feel a bit like a rebellion. Questions about identity and belonging are very significant during the teenage years and your daughter may be wondering about her birth father and her origins, as well as rethinking her relationship with you and questioning the role of your partner. Setting rules with teenagers can be a challenge in most families and you have the extra challenge about her identity to consider.

DISCIPLINE IN BLENDED FAMILIES

To resolve things, I would make a number of suggestions. Firstly, it is worth rethinking and examining your own expectations. If your partner has not had a discipline role up until now, then it might be unrealistic for him to adopt this as she becomes a teenager. Generally in blended families it is okay for you, as the birth parent, to take the main disciplinarian role and for your partner to be in a support role.

You should insist that your daughter displays respect to your partner (and vice versa), but making decisions about rules and boundaries is mainly your responsibility. You should also chat through these issues with your partner and explore what his expectations are. It may be a relief to him that he does not have to be the main disciplinarian, and that he can mainly focus on being supportive towards you and your daughter.

RAISING THE ISSUES WITH YOUR DAUGHTER

It is worth sitting down and trying to talk to your daughter about the issues. Ask her about how she is feeling about things in the family at the moment and directly raise the issue about how she sees your partner and his role in the family. Then you can share your hopes and expectations (for example, that you hope they will continue to get on and that you expect her to be respectful and not rude towards him).

At an appropriate time, bring up a conversation about her birth father. Check how she is feeling about this and whether she wants any more information about the past or even if she wants to make contact at some point in the future. The more you can be open and listen to her about this, the better it will be for her in the long term.

KEEP YOUR RELATIONSHIP WITH YOUR DAUGHTER POSITIVE

As much as possible, try to keep your relationship with your daughter positive. Make sure you have one-to-one time with her during the day, when you chat and enjoy each other's company. Though this can be harder when children become teenagers, it is important – the more you maintain a connection and keep your relationship positive, the easier it will be to resolve discipline issues.

Pay attention to the interests you have in common, what things you enjoy doing together and when you have the best chats, and make sure to build on these. It is equally important for your partner to continue to cultivate his relationship with your daughter, while taking into account that she is now a teenager and may be questioning his role in the family.

MENTAL HEALTH ISSUES

My son has very low self-esteem

Q. *My fourteen-year-old son seems to have very low self-esteem and I am wondering how best to help him. He works hard at school and gets reasonable grades but he is very hard on himself and thinks he is the 'worst' in the class. He takes an interest in sports and GAA in particular. He puts in the commitment and goes to training every week, attending all the matches, but he feels he is always on the B team, fighting for a place. He seems to have no confidence at all. Last night, he got very upset, saying he thought he was no good at anything or that he was only average. When I try to reassure him or praise him about his success at school, he just rejects what I say. It breaks my heart to see him like this.*

A. Many children and teenagers suffer from a lack of confidence and poor self-esteem. This can be particularly upsetting for parents, as it is hard to witness your child expressing such negative feelings towards himself and not recognising his own abilities.

There are many sources of poor self-esteem. Personality factors play a role, with children who have a perfectionist streak frequently being self-critical and negative when they don't reach the high standards they set themselves. Sometimes poor self-esteem is caused by children not having found their niche in life or an arena that matches their strengths and talents. Certainly, self-esteem suffers when children are in overly competitive environments that don't facilitate the expression of their best talents and abilities and where their weaknesses in relationship to others is highlighted. This is a problem for many children in school, where an over-emphasis is put on academic learning which may not be their forte.

In addition, poor self-esteem can be aggravated for children by not having close friends who value and appreciate them. Certainly, one or two close friends who share similar interests can make an enormous difference to a child's self-esteem. The teen years can be a particularly challenging time for a child's confidence, when there is more pressure to fit in and to appear to succeed.

HELPING YOUR SON

There are a number of things you can do to help your son. First of all, it is great he is talking to you about how he feels rather than bottling it up or expressing his frustrations in misbehaviour. The important thing is to always listen to him and to help him talk about how he feels. Reassurance is, of course, important but make sure you don't dismiss his feelings or close down what he is saying.

Be careful about over-praising results or success, especially in the arenas he feels unsuccessful. In these situations it might be best to praise his positive qualities rather than his positive results. For example, you can praise his great commitment to his sport and the fact he turns up each week and tries his best. You can praise his effort in school and his desire to do well. You can even praise aspects of his perfectionistic streak, or at least the positive intentions: 'You really want to get things right, even though it puts you under pressure. That is admirable.'

COMMUNICATING YOUR BELIEF IN HIM

The crucial thing to communicate is that you believe in him, that you think he has great talents and that you enjoy his many positive qualities. Even if you don't communicate this belief directly, he will sense it from you and this will be a great boost to his self-esteem and will help counteract any negative messages he might be receiving.

HELPING HIM FIND HIS NICHE

It is important to help your son find his niche and the activities which he enjoys and allow him to express his talents. Despite best intentions his school work or sport do not seem to be providing this at the moment.

Simple changes might make a difference, such as shifting the emphasis in his school work to subjects he enjoys more or is more successful at. Or you could consider encouraging switching his sporting team to one where he is not 'fighting for his place' but rather that matches his ability level or where he feels more part of the team.

In addition, search out other activities and interests he might enjoy more. You are looking for things that both invoke his passion and interest and which also match his talents and strengths. These don't have to be ones that involve dramatic achievement or success (indeed it might be an idea to steer clear of these) but rather simple things he might enjoy such as playing music, reading, cooking, DIY, gardening, etc. Even learning ordinary household chores and skills can make a young person feel good about themselves.

ENCOURAGING VOLUNTARY WORK AND SOCIAL CONTRIBUTION

You could also consider encouraging your son to undertake voluntary work that might interest him. Often young people are idealistic and want to make a difference. Engaging in voluntary or community work not only allows them to contribute meaningfully in a way that helps others – it is also likely to be a boost to their self-esteem and confidence. For example, you could consider encouraging him to participate in An Gaisce, the President's Award, which encourages young people to undertake personal challenges in arenas such as learning personal skills, recreation, venture and community involvement. The great thing about the Gaisce process is that it is not competitive – the young person sets their personal challenges that fit their own personality and then commits to achieve them. During the process they have the opportunity to meet new people, learn new skills and make new friends.

My fifteen-year-old seems to be depressed

Q. *I would like to ask for your help or advice in relation to a major problem that we have with our youngest child. He is just fifteen and due to sit his Junior Cert this June. He is a quiet child by nature and never had a lot of, if any, self-confidence, no matter how well he excelled at anything. In the past year or so he has lost all interest in sport, does no homework, has no close friends, and seems to have withdrawn into himself and I would say has become mildly depressed. He is just like a lost child now, with no focus or direction, and there is no talking or reasoning with him. We have three older children, two girls and one boy, and all of them would have suffered from lack of self-confidence and self-esteem. This is especially true of my eldest daughter, who is in her twenties, suffering from depression and on medication for some years now. We are worried that the fifteen year old is beginning to show similar traits. Could you recommend somebody we could go to to get our son assessed and see if we can get some help for him before it is too late?*

A. During adolescence it is much more common for children to experience feelings of low mood or to become depressed at times. This is partly due to the turmoil of adolescence which, along with hormones and physical changes, brings a rollercoaster of intense emotions and moods. In addition, adolescents experience many more stresses and strains, whether it is the increased pressure to study or do well in exams, learning how to fit in with peers, or working out big questions of their own self-identity. Adolescents naturally question the values of the adult world and what really matters in life and this can lead some to become a bit alienated or rebellious. While such issues are relatively common in adolescence, a small number of young people can become depressed and, in serious cases, this can affect their motivation and disrupt their participation in ordinary life.

Young people who lack confidence, who have fewer friends or who live in families where there is a history of depression are particularly at risk. For these reasons you are right to be concerned about your son and to be thinking about how best to help him.

GETTING PROFESSIONAL HELP

Professional help may be of benefit and you could consider taking your son to your local Child and Adolescent Mental Health Service (you should be able to get a referral from your GP or via your son's school). Such a service should be able to provide you with an assessment of your son's needs and a recommended treatment plan. Different treatments can be of benefit, including individual or group counselling, family therapy, medication, as well as providing support for you as his parents to manage the situation.

You may also be able to access support through your son's school, where there might be an attached counsellor or psychologist or, alternatively, you may be able to access a private therapist from an organisation such as the Psychological Society of Ireland, Irish Association for Counselling and Psychotherapy or Irish Council of Psychotherapy (all of which can easily be found online). Make sure to seek a therapist who is experienced in working with young people and their families.

WHAT THERAPY HELPS

The type of therapy that is most often recommended for depression is cognitive behavioural therapy, which would focus on helping your son identify and challenge negative patterns of thinking, and on planning constructive behaviours. However, the truth is that the approach that will work best is the one that most appeals to your son and the one he will most engage in. The key is finding a therapist or approach that clicks with your son and gets him engaged and motivated to make positive changes.

WHAT PARENTS CAN DO

There is also a lot you can do as parents to help your son, and in studies it is parental support that is most highly rated in getting young people through difficult times. The key is getting the balance right between listening to and supporting your son as well as challenging him and putting gentle pressure on him to get out and do things.

This means that at times it is important to encourage him to open up and talk about how he is feeling and at other times to gently encourage him to take action to make changes. The ideal is to get your son on board and to work together on small achievable goals. For example, you might start by focusing on doing some study, picking a favourite or easy subject, or you might make a plan for your son to go out on a trip to meet a friend or to make a small step towards restarting a sport or other helpful interest. Even simple things like helping your son prepare a family dinner can make a difference. Being patient and setting small goals is crucial.

MAINTAIN YOUR RELATIONSHIP WITH YOUR SON

It is also important that you maintain your relationship with your son. Try not to be on his back all the time and make sure there are other times of lighter or even 'neutral' conversation when you can chat with him about ordinary things (like TV programmes or a football match). The ideal is to try to do some enjoyable daily activities together, whether this is taking a walk, driving him somewhere or preparing lunch together. A good connection with you as his parent will make a big difference to his well-being in the long term.

LIVING WITH SOMEONE WHO IS DEPRESSED

Living with someone who is down or depressed can be difficult for the family. As well as the worry as to how your son is doing, it can be hard work trying to motivate him and to make strides to get things done. In addition, although depression can mainly present as low mood, it can also be expressed by the young person as irritation, boredom or even anger and this can be hard to manage. As a result, it is important as parents to seek support yourselves, both for your own well-being and so you can be energised to help your son.

You might find some more information in a book I have written with Professor Carol Fitzpatrick, *Coping with Depression in Young People: A Guide for Parents* (see Further Reading for full details).

My fourteen-year-old is always anxious

Q. *My fourteen-year-old daughter has always been an anxious child who would let worries get to her. For a lot of her childhood she was afraid of the dark and going places alone and we would have to reassure her a lot (and often let her sleep in bed with us). For a few years she was acutely afraid of dogs and then this lessened. I had hoped she was growing out of her fears but she continues to be a big worrier and I notice that she often avoids doing things she might like because of her fears. For example, she dropped out of a school play due to performance anxiety and also didn't go on an overnight stay with a couple of friends a week ago, which I know was due to her being fearful about sleeping at night in a new place. It is very hard to reason with her about her worries and sometimes we have these long conversations that can end with both of us upset. What can we do to help her? I don't want her to go through life missing out on things because of her anxiety.*

A. Anxiety and worrying excessively are amongst the most common mental health problems for children and adults and many people have an inclination to worry and ruminate from time to time. How much of it is a problem depends on how much the worrying impacts a person's life and stops them getting on with everyday things. Like your daughter, many children get into a pattern of avoiding the feared situation in order to stop feeling anxious. However, this causes them to not only miss out on important life experiences but stops them learning how to handle their anxiety, which may be more intense the next time a similar situation comes round as a result. The good news is that you can do a lot to help children and teenagers manage their anxiety and to stop it interfering in their lives.

LISTEN AND SUPPORT YOUR CHILD
Firstly, it is important to understand and be supportive when your child is worried. It is very helpful for a child to express their worries and for someone to sympathetically understand their feelings without dismissing or judging them. Acknowledging anxious feelings is very important and helps a child realise that these feelings are normal and that they can be overcome and managed.

DON'T GET CAUGHT UP IN THE WORRY
However, it is also important not to get hooked into your child's worries nor to collude with them or spend too much time discussing them. It is very easy to get caught into a long discussion with a child trying to argue them out of their worry, exploring a long sequences of what ifs. The danger of such long conversations is that they can increase a child's ruminations and this may end in frustration. One of the most important strategies I use with parents and anxious children is to keep discussions about worries limited to specific times and to specific durations. For younger children

this time can be a fifteen-minute 'worry time', or with teenagers it can be simply your chat before bed. Such an approach takes the worries seriously but helps keep them contained.

KEEP YOUR OWN ANXIETY AND FRUSTRATION CONTAINED

Many children who are anxious have anxious parents. A child's fears can cause their parents to become anxious and worried in response. Alternatively, it is easy to get frustrated listening to a child's worries – you might start out by listening and being reassuring and then eventually end up being frustrated and angry as they continue to ruminate. The important thing is to try and contain your own feelings – the more calm and supportive you are, the better. In addition, take a break before you get frustrated: 'Let's step away from this for a while and talk again after dinner.

HELP YOUR CHILD ADDRESS THE PROBLEM SITUATION

Some of your daughter's worries can be solved or the situation can be changed to make it more manageable. You can brainstorm with her about how you can negotiate the sleepover and how she might successfully approach performing in the school play. Frequently, anxious children have good problem-solving abilities and imaginations, but often these strengths are employed against them as they visualise all the things that can go wrong. You want to help your daughter redirect these strengths to overcome the problem, whether this is imagining things going well, identifying what she needs to do to prepare and strategising about the best approach to a social situation.

HELP YOUR CHILD MANAGE THEIR ANXIETY

It is also important to help your child learn to manage their anxious feelings so that they don't feel overwhelmed by them. There are many different strategies that can be learnt to achieve this, such as becoming mindful of the anxious feelings in your body or using your breath to relax. Alternatively, you can help your daughter learn to distract herself from worries, for example by focusing on the task in hand, by visualising a positive outcome, by building a picture in her mind of a safe place, or by repeating positive coping statements such as, 'This is fine, I can get through this' before going into an anxious situation.

In addition, certain creative rituals can also help, such as writing worries out on a page (rather than ruminating about them at night) and then placing them in a 'worry box' to be dealt with in the morning.

There are lots of good books and resources online that deal with strategies to overcome worries. You could read these books and learn these strategies with your daughter, or alternatively seek out relaxation or yoga classes that you could attend together. Working together as a team to overcome anxiety could also be great for your relationship with your daughter.

The key to overcoming anxiety is to accept and understand your anxious feelings, to use them as a call to action and to break the pattern of avoidance. You want to help your daughter to learn 'to feel the fear and do it anyway'. If it continues to be a problem, seek help from an adolescent mental health or counselling service.

My nineteen-year-old daughter has an eating disorder

Q. *My nineteen-year-old daughter was diagnosed with an eating disorder about nine months ago and has been attending a clinic on an outpatient basis ever since. Although she has made some progress, my husband and I are increasingly worried about her as she refuses to eat the required amount of food the clinic recommends and is very underweight. I have made several attempts to encourage her and although sometimes it seems I am getting the message across about how important it is for her to look after herself properly, ultimately she is really struggling to consume normal amounts of food. I am at the end of my tether. Do you have any advice? I feel this is an important issue which needs to be faced more openly by society. I do not wish any other parent to have to endure what I and my husband do.*

A. Unfortunately, eating disorders such as anorexia or bulimia are common in western countries, with between 1 per cent and 3 per cent of young women meeting the criteria for diagnosis and up to 10 per cent having some form of eating problem. Such disorders are particularly worrying due to their serious physical health implications. The sufferer can be dangerously underweight, which leads to an increased risk of a whole range of illnesses and complications. Your question highlights the plight of families of those with eating disorders, who are very worried about their loved one, yet struggle with knowing how best to help.

UNDERSTANDING YOUR DAUGHTER'S PROBLEMS

In helping your daughter, it is important to understand what is going on for her and how the disorder affects her. An eating disorder can start out innocently as a diet, as the young person begins to control and restrict their eating. Over time, however, this habit becomes all-consuming, with the person constantly obsessing about food and their body shape. Their compulsion to restrict their eating becomes fixed and less within their control. Frequently, sufferers get into the habit of controlling their eating as a means of managing stress or difficult feelings – they control their eating as other things in their life are less easy to control.

For many, an eating disorder is like an addiction. Though the person knows on one level that restricting their eating is harmful, they are literally addicted to their compulsive habits. It is very hard for them to break the habit of constantly ruminating about food and restricting their eating. Overcoming an addiction can present many challenges but it can be done with support and a willingness to try.

WORKING TOGETHER WITH YOUR DAUGHTER TO TACKLE THE EATING DISORDER

The first step to helping your daughter is to get her cooperation and to make sure you are working together to tackle her eating disorder. As a parent it is easy to get into a battle with her as you encourage her to eat the correct amount of food. The disorder can make her resist these attempts, thwart your plans and increase the conflict between you.

It can help if you view the disorder as external to your daughter, much like a disease that you are working together to overcome. Your conflict is with the disorder and not with your daughter. In concrete terms, this means trying to agree goals with her about when, how and what she will eat, and to see yourselves working as a team to achieve this. The key is to make goals very small and to build on any signs of progress. If the simple goal of eating an apple for breakfast is progress, then this should be marked and celebrated.

SEEKING PROFESSIONAL HELP AND SUPPORT

Attending the outpatient clinic can help with this, as the staff can be outside arbitrators to give your daughter feedback on the seriousness of her problem and motivate her to set goals that you can both work on.

A range of individual, family and group therapies might help, depending on your daughter's specific needs. A cognitive behavioural approach, for example, would focus on helping your daughter challenge her distorted beliefs about body shape and her unhelpful eating habits, while setting positive concrete behavioural goals to overcome them. This can help, but the most important thing is to find empathic mental health professionals you can work with.

There are also a number of voluntary sector services such as BodyWhys (www.bodywhys.ie), which offers helpline and group support for individuals and their families, or Overeaters Anonymous (www.overeatersanonymous.ie), which follows a twelve-step group approach to recovery. Through these organisations, try to make contact with other parents dealing with similar issues as this can be a crucial source of support and information.

Be careful to monitor your daughter's weight and health, and continue to work closely with health professionals as needed: if things deteriorate, be prepared to step up her level of care as needed. Many people with eating disorders can benefit from inpatient treatment, especially if their weight becomes dangerously low. A residential stay can be used as a time to kick-start a period of recovery.

In addition, make sure to consider alternative therapies such as relaxation, yoga or mindfulness, all of which could contribute to improving her health.

FOCUS ON POSITIVE LIFE GOALS

As well as focusing on tackling the eating disorder and setting small goals around healthy eating, it is important to support your daughter in getting on with her life, whether this is in pursuing study or employment, making friends, having relationships and doing what you would expect other nineteen-year-old girls to be doing.

When you have an eating disorder, it can take centre stage and prevent you from getting on with your life – which can make things much worse. Indeed, what often helps a young person overcome their disorder in the long term is achieving in other areas of their lives, whether this be working in a satisfying career, establishing quality friendships and relationships, making a contribution in voluntary work or taking up interesting leisure activities or pastimes.

I'm worried about teen suicide

Q. *The many suicides of young people reported in the media have made me really worried as a parent. I have two teenagers, a boy who is fourteen and a girl who is sixteen. As far as I know they are doing well, with the usual ups and downs of teenage years. But sometimes I worry if I could be missing something. How could I tell if they were in distress or even suicidal? I don't want to be morbid, but you read in the newspapers how frequently the suicide came out of the blue and the parents never suspected a thing. How can you spot the early warning signs as a parent? You also read about copycat suicides, which is terrifying. Should I talk to my children about what is going on in the media, and if so, how should I go about it? I don't want to make matters worse or, worse still, put ideas in their head.*

A. Though the media coverage about the tragic suicides of young people can raise important issues, there is the danger that some of the reporting can inadvertently present suicide as a legitimate or even heroic choice for young people in distress. Given the potential for copycat or clustering of suicides, it matters greatly how suicides are reported in the media and how they are discussed with young people in schools and families in particular. When suicide prevention programmes were being developed for schools in the USA, many of the initial evaluations found that some programmes (which focused on providing information and educating young people about suicide) did not reduce the incidence of suicide and may have actually increased young people's thinking about it as an option. The key learning from these initial programmes is that raising the subject of suicide is a delicate conversation to get right with young people and that prevention should largely focus on positive mental health and equipping your children to deal with distress appropriately.

TALKING TO YOUR TEENAGERS ABOUT SUICIDE

When the subject of suicide comes up in the media or if your teenager hears of a suicide in their local area, it is important that you discuss the issue with them, rather than keeping silent. Take the view that as teenagers they will have discussed it with their peers and it is important that you as their parents are also involved in this conversation. The first thing to do is acknowledge the tragedy of what has happened and give them space to share their thoughts and feelings. Then make sure to acknowledge the distress and upset the young person must have been feeling in this situation, and how particularly sad it was that they did not talk to someone or recognise the other options they had to tackle their problems. Crucially, you should also make sure to acknowledge the enormous distress for the young person's family and friends and to help your teenager empathise with this. Talk of how serious and irreversible suicide is and the great harm suicide does to a family, the community and society. The key message that you want your teenager to take away is that suicide causes great harm to other people as well as the young person and is never a legitimate option to dealing with distress. While being sensitive and empathic, you want your teenager to realise that the 'heroic' course of action for someone in distress is to deal with their problems and to continue to live, despite their suffering, for the sake of themselves and those close to them.

SUICIDE PREVENTION

The suicide prevention programmes in schools that show the most potential are the ones that emphasise positive mental health, active coping strategies when dealing with problems and reaching out to others and talking when in distress.

In the same spirit, it is useful to adopt a similar approach with your own children. Sit down and talk with them about the importance of looking after their own mental health, in particular emphasising the importance of talking to someone when under pressure or stressed. Remind them that you are always there to listen, no matter what is upsetting them, whether trivial or serious. Make sure to practice this openness as a parent, developing the habit of listening first to your teenager – even if you have just had a row or they have done something wrong, and especially if they are embarrassed about talking.

EXPLORE COPING STRATEGIES
It can be particularly helpful to explore with teenagers what coping strategies they might employ when under stress or dealing with a difficult situation. For example, you could talk with them about who they might talk to if they were feeling down about a problem (in addition to yourself) or how they would reach out to a friend they thought might be feeling down.

There are particular risk factors associated with teenagers harming themselves, such as engaging in drinking, drug taking or other risky behaviours, particularly within an unsupportive peer group. It is important to do what you can as a parent to reduce these risks by encouraging their more supportive friendships that are a good influence. It is also important to explore how they can respond to difficult situations. For example, you could ask them how they might say no if another teenager who had been drinking offered them a lift home. Your aim is to build the range of good strategies they can draw upon in these difficult situations.

KEEP CONNECTED TO YOUR TEENAGER
Each teenager is different and the early warning signals that a teenager might be in distress varies greatly. The key as a parent is to stay connected and tuned in so you can notice any changes that indicate problems, such as becoming cut off or uncommunicative, appearing under stress or having

friendship or relationship problems. Then you can take steps to reach out and support them. For some related articles on supporting teenagers in distress or when suicidal, please see my website www.solutiontalk.ie.

FURTHER READING

From the Same Author

Fitzpatrick, C. and J. Sharry, *Coping with Depression in Young People: A Guide for Parents*, Chichester: Wiley, 2004.

Sharry, J., *Bringing Up Responsible Teenagers*, Dublin: Veritas, 2008.

Sharry, J., *Counselling Children, Adolescents and Families: A Strengths-Based Collaborative Approach*, London: Sage, 2004.

Sharry, J., *Parent Power*, Chichester: Wiley, 2002.

Sharry, J., *Solution Focused Groupwork*, second edition, London: Sage, 2008.

Sharry J., G. Hampson and M. Fanning, *Parenting Preschoolers and Young Children*, Dublin: Veritas, 2005.

Sharry, J., B. Madden and M. Darmody, *Becoming A Solution-Focused Detective: Identifying your Clients' Strengths in Brief Therapy*, second edition, London: Routledge, 2011.

Sharry, J., P. Reid and E. Donohoe, *When Parents Separate: A Guide to Helping You and Your Children Cope*, Dublin: Veritas, 2001.

Other Books for Parents

Covey, S. R., *The Seven Habits of Highly Effective Families*, London: Simon and Schuster, 1997.

Gottman, J., *The Heart of Parenting: How to Raise an Emotionally Intelligent Child*, London: Bloomsbury, 1997.

Nelson, J. and L. Lott, *Positive Discipline for Teenagers*, Roseville, California: Prima Publishing, 2000.

Quinn, M. and T. Quinn, *What Can a Parent of a Teenager Do?* Newry: Family Caring Trust, 1988.

For Group Leaders

1. Sharry, J. and C. Fitzpatrick, *Parents Plus Children's Programme: A Video-Based Parenting Guide to Managing Behaviour Problems and*